The Children's Encyclopedia
of BIBLE TIMES

Written by Mark Water
Illustrations by Karen Donnelly

ZondervanPublishingHouse
Grand Rapids, Michigan

A Division of HarperCollins*Publishers*

THE CHILDREN'S ENCYCLOPEDIA OF
BIBLE TIMES

COPYRIGHT © 1995 HUNT & THORPE
TEXT © MARK WATER
ILLUSTRATIONS © KAREN DONNELLY

Originally published by Hunt & Thorpe 1995

Designed by
THE BRIDGEWATER BOOK COMPANY
Designer *Sarah Bentley*
Managing Editor *Anna Clarkson*
Editor *Fiona Corbridge*
Page make-up *Chris Lanaway*
Text consultant *Derek Williams*

ISBN 0-310-21103-4

In the United States this book is published by:
Zondervan Publishing House
Grand Rapids, Michigan 49530

ACKNOWLEDGEMENTS
Bible quotations are from:
The Holy Bible, New International Version,
© 1973, 1978, 1984 by International Bible
Society. Used by permission of Hodder and
Stoughton. International Children's Bible, New
Century Version (Anglicized Edition),
© 1991 Word (UK) Ltd. Used by permission.

CONTENTS

ABOUT THIS BOOK

This book is like a dictionary. All the subjects are in alphabetical order. This means that you don't have to start at the beginning: you can start anywhere, depending on what you want to read about. The title at the top of each page gives you the main subject for that page. You can find which page you need by looking in the contents page, or in the index at the end of this book.

The Bible was written by many different people over a long period of time. This book tells you about everyday life in Bible times: how people looked, what they wore, what their homes were like.

Enjoy the colourful, clearly drawn artwork – it shows you what people wore in Bible times, how they lived and travelled, and also what we think the different characters might have looked like.

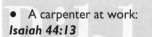

Bible Search

- A carpenter at work: *Isaiah 44:13*

- A lost axe-head: *2 Kings 6:5–7*

- Foreign carpenters and stonemasons: *2 Samuel 5:11*

- Tearing up a roof to see Jesus: *Mark 2:4*

When you read these pages you may think, 'Does the Bible really say that?' The best thing you can do is to find out for yourself! Most of the pages have a Bible Search so that you can look up the verses in your own Bible.

ANY QUESTIONS

These questions help you examine the text more closely, and to think about some of the Bible's teachings.

On many pages you will see the words 'See also' or 'To find out more'. By turning to the suggested pages, you can follow a story or a subject through the book. For example, read about Idols, then turn to Worship, and then to Psalm 150, and so on.

THE BIBLE
There are 66 books in the Bible. This may seem like a lot of pages, but there is an easy system for finding your way around:

- Each Bible book is split up into chapters, and each chapter has a number. Exodus 1 means the first chapter of the Book of Exodus. Usually these numbers are set at the top of each page in your Bible.
- Each chapter is split up into short sections of one or two lines. These are called verses. Verses also have numbers. The verse numbers are the small numbers on each page. So Exodus 1:12 means verse 12 of chapter 1 of the Book of Exodus.

BC refers to all the years before Jesus was born: 500 BC means 500 years before Jesus was born. AD refers to all the years after Jesus was born.
All the dates of events in the Old Testament are 'BC'; all the dates in the New Testament are 'AD'.

Fox

Rock hyrax

ANIMALS WILD

T he Bible refers to over seventy different animals: farm animals, working animals and wild animals. You can still see many of these in Israel today. Others, such as lions, bears and wild oxen, no longer live there.

MOUNTAIN ANIMALS

Ibex

Lion

DOGS, FOXES AND JACKALS

In Palestine, dogs were despised. If you wanted to insult someone, you said, 'You dog!'

Dogs ran wild and carried diseases because they hunted among the rubbish tips for food. These wild dogs could be scared off with a stick.

Foxes hunted alone. Besides killing small animals, they spoiled crops by eating fruit and damaging grape vines.

Jackals hunted in packs, scavenging for scraps of food.

Dog

The mountain goat, or ibex, lived in rocky mountainous areas. Males had large, backward-curving horns.

The rock hyrax, also known as cony or rock badger, was a small shy animal about the size of a rabbit. It lived in groups in holes on the mountainside. Powerful suction pads on its feet helped it to cling to the steepest rocks.

Gazelles were common. They were only 60 cm (2 ft) high and 1 m (3 ft) long. Some girls were named Dorcas, meaning 'gazelle'.

LIONS, LEOPARDS AND BEARS

Lions had short curly manes and were smaller than African lions. They killed sheep and sometimes people.

Leopards were feared even more than lions, as they seemed more intelligent and savage. Their spotted coats were a perfect camouflage.

Syrian brown bears roamed the hills of Israel.

Leopards

- Samson and 300 jackals: *Judges 15:4-5*
- David kills a lion and bear: *1 Samuel 17:34-35*
- Ibex and rock hyrax: *Psalm 104:18*
- Mountain goat: *Job 39:1, 1 Samuel 24:2*

Bear

ANIMALS FARM AND WORKING

People and animals lived and worked together. Animals were not usually kept as pets. In the New Testament, there is one reference to small dogs under a table, which could be pet dogs. And in the Old Testament, we can read about a pet lamb.

Donkey

ANIMAL TRAVEL

Today we have cars, but in Bible times, people used animals to travel around. Many families had a donkey. They could travel 30 km (19 miles) a day. Kings rode on donkeys when they wanted to show that they came in peace.

Horses were only owned by kings and warriors.

Although they were bad-tempered and stubborn, camels were perfect for travelling in the desert. Their humps stored fat. They could go for a week without drinking, as each of their three stomachs held 23 litres (13 pints) of water. Long eyelashes protected their eyes from sand. The Arabian camel (a one-humped fast riding camel) could travel 100 km (160 miles) in a day.

SHEEP

Sheep's wool was used to make warm clothes. Their skins were tanned for leather, and their horns were turned into musical instruments and jugs for oil. (To find out more, turn to the page on Shepherds.)

Lambs were important for sacrifices. You can read about this on the page on Sacrifices.

Horse and chariot

GOATS

Goats could eat twigs and leaves. This made them easier to keep than sheep, which only ate grass. Goats' strong black hair was woven into ropes and cloth for tents. Their skins were made into water-bottles.

Water-bottle

• A pet lamb:
2 Samuel 12: 1-4

• A journey with camels:
Genesis 24: 10-33

• Sheep and goats together:
Matthew 25: 31-33

• A market for animals:
John 2: 13-16

Sheep

CATTLE

Cattle were kept for their milk, meat and skins. Bulls, cows and especially oxen were used to pull wagons, plough fields and thresh grain.

Milking a cow

6

BEGGARS AND LEPERS

There were no hospitals in Bible times, and no hostels, pensions, unemployment benefits or state aid. So people who were disabled, or too ill to work, had to beg. There were many beggars and lepers in Palestine in the time of Jesus.

A beggar

HELP YOURSELF

The law said that it was the duty of every Jew to give money and food to beggars. Every farmer had to leave corn on the edges of his fields, and fruit on his trees, and poor people and beggars were allowed to help themselves. However, it was forbidden for the poor to take a sickle to the cornfields, or a basket to the orchards, probably so that they couldn't take too much!

Beggars were allowed to take food from farmers

Bible Search

- Old Testament lepers: *Leviticus 13:45–46*
- Jesus heals a leper: *Mark 1:40–44*
- Bartimaeus: *Mark 10:46–52*

BLIND BARTIMAEUS

Jesus was passing through Jericho when a voice in the crowd shouted out, 'Son of David, have mercy on me!' It was a blind beggar called Bartimaeus, sitting by the roadside. 'Be quiet!' people hissed at Bartimaeus, but Jesus stopped. Bartimaeus felt his way to Jesus. 'What do you want me to do?' Jesus asked. 'Teacher, I want to see,' replied Bartimaeus. Jesus said, 'Your faith has healed you,' and Bartimaeus was able to see.

Bartimaeus

LEPROSY

In the Bible the word 'leprosy' is used for a number of skin diseases. Many of the skin diseases could be cured, but real leprosy was incurable, and slowly killed the sufferer. Today, doctors know how to cure leprosy.

Leprosy was infectious, so lepers had to live apart from everybody else. They were allowed to live together in groups to help each other.

There were laws to make sure that everyone knew who had leprosy. Lepers had to:
- Tear their clothes.
- Leave their head uncovered, and not brush their hair.
- Cover the lower part of their face.
- Call 'Unclean! Unclean!' whenever they saw anyone.

Lepers

7

BIRDS
IN THE BIBLE

I srael has over 350 species of bird, although the Bible only mentions about fifty. People called many different types of bird by the same name: 'twitterers' (often translated as 'sparrow').

- Eagle: *Deuteronomy 32:10–11*
- Raven: *I Kings 17:4*
- Holy Spirit like the dove: *John 1:32*
- Migrating birds: *Jeremiah 8:7*

Bible Search

SYMBOLIC BIRDS

In stories, the vulture often represented judgment. The powerful eagle swooping down to catch its young on its wings made people think of God's loving care. Owls were often used as a symbol of loneliness. Doves belong to the pigeon family. They are strong birds, able to fly long distances. They are gentle and loving, keeping one mate for life. Doves were the most important bird in the Bible. They were the only bird that could be offered as a sacrifice. A dove was God's symbol for the Holy Spirit.

WAITERS AND ALARM CLOCKS

The Hebrew word for raven means any large black bird. Ravens were once God's waiters, bringing food to Elijah. Cockerels were reliable alarm clocks in the morning.

Raven

Vulture

Cockerel

Owl

BIRDS ON HOLIDAY

Birds have highways in the air, just as we have highways on land. Israel lies under a busy air route for birds. Each autumn and spring, Israel is a stopping-off place for many thousands of migrating birds.

BIRTH AND BABIES

Babies were thought of as a gift from God. The more you had the happier you were. But people thought that it was better to have baby boys than to have baby girls. When girls got married, they belonged to another family. But boys stayed with their parents and earned money. Parents felt they lived on through their sons.

A father and his son

BIRTH

Babies were born at home, with the help of a midwife. As soon as a baby was born it was washed, and rubbed with salt. The baby was wrapped in a cloth and then in strips of cloth. These were called swaddling clothes. Mothers thought that it made the baby's body grow strong and straight. When a baby boy was born, there was often a small party every night for a week. This was followed by a big party on the eighth day.

Salt

Party food

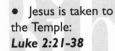

Bible Search

● Jesus is taken to the Temple:
Luke 2:21-38

● John the Baptist is named:
Luke 1:59-66

● Midwives who cared:
Exodus 1:15-21

A party for a new baby

CIRCUMCISION

After eight days, every baby boy had a small piece of skin cut off from the end of his penis. This was a sign that he belonged to God and to God's people, the Jews. There was sometimes a small religious service to thank God for a baby girl.

NAMES

In Old Testament times, people thought your name had power over you. It was chosen carefully. By the time of the New Testament, a son was usually given his grandfather's name. He was also called 'the son of' ('Ben' or 'Bar') his father. There were no surnames. Boys were probably named when they were circumcised.

PRESENTATION IN THE TEMPLE

The first boy to be born into a family was considered to belong to God. So when the baby was a month old, his parents went to the Temple to make an offering to God and 'buy back' the baby boy. They took two pigeons for a sacrifice, and paid five silver coins.

CARPENTERS AND BUILDERS

Joseph teaches Jesus carpentry

arpenters were important men in village life. They made and mended furniture, tools, stairs, chariots and door-posts. They also helped the local builder to put up the simple village houses. Before the Romans introduced benches, carpenters would sit on the ground to work outside their homes.

Jesus' father, Joseph, trained Jesus to be a carpenter.

A carpenter at work

TOOLS

Carpenters had a variety of tools. Axes were used for cutting down trees. Axe-heads were first made of bronze, and later of iron. The head was tied to a shaft. Trees were cut into logs with a saw.

To hammer things, a carpenter would probably use a stone. Nails were first made of bronze, and later of iron.

To bore a hole, a tool called an awl was used. Carpenters also had chisels and planes for shaping and smoothing wood. Builders used a plumbline to make sure a wall was straight.

Bible search

- A carpenter at work: *Isaiah 44:13*
- A lost axe-head: *2 Kings 6:5–7*
- Foreign carpenters and stonemasons: *2 Samuel 5:11*
- Tearing up a roof to see Jesus: *Mark 2:4*

HOUSES

Village houses were usually made of mud bricks. To make a roof, a carpenter laid beams of wood across the top of a house, and filled the gaps with reeds or straw and mud.

Building a house

ANY QUESTIONS

1 How did a carpenter prepare wood for building a house?
2 What type of buildings were made from stone?

STONE BUILDINGS

Workers in stone made city walls, storage silos, wells, cisterns (pits for holding rainwater), arches, tunnels, and important buildings. It was hard, skilled work.

Splitting limestone

BUILDING WITH LIMESTONE

Large blocks of limestone were broken into smaller blocks. This is how it was done. A line of holes was chipped out with a chisel and hammer. Wooden pegs were stuck in the holes, and water was poured over the stone and wood. The wood soaked up the water, got larger, and broke the stone. The blocks of stone were then smoothed with a plane, so that they would fit together without mortar.

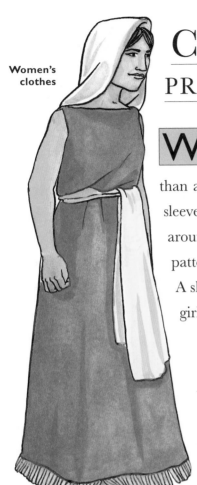

Women's clothes

CLOTHES FOR WOMEN, PRAYER AND THE RICH

W omen's clothes were similar to men's. The inner garment was fuller and longer, and the outer tunic would be longer than a man's. It might have a fringe to cover the feet, pointed sleeves, or no sleeves at all. Many tunics had embroidery around the neck, and each village had its own special patterns. Women often wore blue.

A shawl was sometimes worn over the head. Unmarried girls would wear a veil. Widows wore a black veil.

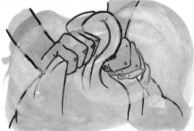

An unmarried girl

CLOTHES FOR PRAYER

Men wore prayer shawls (called a tallith) with a tassel at each corner, and phylacteries on their forehead and left arm. These were little boxes containing Old Testament laws.

A phylactery

Some prophets, such as John the Baptist, wore one garment which was a cloak and tunic in one. It was made of woven camelhair, and was tied at the waist with a leather belt.

WASHING CLOTHES

Clothes were washed in running water in a stream. The water dislodged the dirt as it flowed through the material. Soap was made from sodium carbonate and fat or olive oil.

See also the pages on Soldiers, Priests, Pharisees, and Make-up.

RICH PEOPLE

The rich wore the same styles as the poor, but made of finer fabrics. Tunics might be made of linen or cotton, and cloaks out of silk. Cloaks often had tassels and blue ribbons at the corners, or fringes round the hem, to remind the wearer to obey God.

A rich person might wear leather shoes, instead of sandals, and a leather belt.

Headgear was elaborate, such as a turban with a fringe. Fine jewellery would be worn too.

Bible Search

- Fringes and tassels: *Numbers 15:38*
- John the Baptist's clothes: *Matthew 3:4*
- A runner: *2 Kings 4:29*
- A rich prize at a wedding: *Judges 14:12*

11

CLOTHES FOR MEN, CLOAKS AND ACCESSORIES

During the two thousand years covered by the Bible, the style of clothes changed very little.

The Jews loved nice clothes, dyed in bright colours. Vertical stripes were popular. Most people wore woollen clothes, or hair-cloth if they were poor, but rich people wore linen or silk. Many people had 'best clothes' as well as everyday clothes. The finest clothes were white.

MEN'S CLOTHES

New tunics were sold without an opening for the head

A man would wear an inner tunic, and another tunic on top. New tunics were sold without an opening for the head, to show that no one had worn them.

In Jesus' time, big looms were invented which allowed tunics to be made in one piece, without any seams.

Belts were made out of a long piece of cloth folded in half and wrapped two or three times round the waist. The folds made a good pocket. At work a man tucked his tunic into his belt, so he could move more easily.

Bible Search

- Jesus' tunic: *John 19:23–24*

- A runner tucks in his cloak: *2 Kings 4:29*

- Don't keep a man's cloak overnight: *Exodus 22:26–27*

CLOAKS

A cloak was used as an overcoat, blanket, and saddle cloth. For most people, a cloak lasted their lifetime. It was their most valuable piece of clothing: without it, people felt they weren't properly dressed.

A working man's cloak was made from two thick woollen blankets sewn at the shoulders, or it might be one large square of cloth with holes for his arms and head.

At night, people took off their belts and slept in their tunics, with their cloak for a blanket.

HEAD TO FOOT

People wore simple sandals, made of a leather base tied to the foot with a thong. These were taken off indoors.

For head coverings, men and women often wore a square of material folded crossways, with the material falling to protect the neck from the sun. It was held in place by a plaited cord.

Some men wore a cloth wound round the head like a turban.

A head covering

CRIME AND PUNISHMENT

To commit a crime is to purposely act in a harmful way. There is crime against God, against people and against property. But for the Jews, all crime was a crime against God, because it broke his command: 'Be holy, for I am holy.'

The Old Testament gave all the laws that had to be kept. The Jews made rules to make sure justice was done. For example, when someone was accused of a crime, there had to be two eye-witnesses.

A stoning

PUNISHMENT

● Death penalty.
This was given for crimes including blasphemy (saying bad things about God), making idols, and adultery. The Jews usually stoned the guilty person to death.

Crucifixion was introduced by the Romans. In the time of Jesus, a death sentence could only be passed by the Romans.

● 'An eye for an eye'.
In Old Testament times, this meant that you could not do more to another person than he had done to you.

By the time of the New Testament, people normally made up for some offences by paying money to the victim. For example, if you left your well uncovered, and a donkey fell in it, you paid the animal's owner.

If a donkey fell in your well, you had to pay its owner

● Flogging.
The Jewish punishment of flogging, or whipping, was not as severe as a Roman flogging. The Romans' whips had lumps of lead or bone on them.

● Prisons.

In Old Testament times, prisons were not really used until after the Jews' exile in Babylonia (although enemies of the king were kept locked up). In New Testament times, prisons were common. People who got into debt were often sent to prison.

ANY QUESTIONS
1 Why did the Jews believe all crimes were crimes against God?
2 Was 'an eye for an eye' a fair rule?

Bible Search

● Justice: *Exodus 23:6–8*
● Fines and payments: *Exodus 22:1–15*
● Stocks: *Jeremiah 20:2*
● Prison: *Jeremiah 32:2, Matthew 5:25, Acts 5:18*
● Flogging and stocks: *Acts 16:22–24*

COURTS

In Old Testament times, a court of law would be held outside, by the city gates. Cases were judged by the city elders.

In New Testament times, the Sanhedrin (a council of religious leaders in Jerusalem) was the main law court. Serious crimes against God were tried here. Smaller courts of law judged less important cases.

A court of law

A mummy

DEATH AND BURIAL

What happens to us when we die? The Egyptians believed that when kings, priests and rich people died, they travelled to a land ruled over by the god Osiris. In many tombs, a boat was laid by the coffin, for the journey. The Egyptians believed that the soul needed a body. So bodies were embalmed, or turned into mummies, to stop them rotting.

PALESTINE

A dead person was washed, and rubbed with sweet-smelling oils. Then the body was wrapped in white cloths. Jewish law said that burial had to take place within eight hours.

Relatives carried the body on a wooden frame to the place of burial. The procession was led by the women. People cried, put ash on their hair, and walked with bare feet. Sometimes they tore their clothes as a sign of grief. Even the poorest families paid for mourners to weep and wail, and had at least two flute players.

A funeral procession

Bible Search

- A family tomb:
  Genesis 50:12–13
- Burial of Jesus:
  John 19:38–42
- Dorcas dies:
  Acts 9:36–39

GRAVES

Only the poorest people were buried in public cemeteries. Most ordinary people had graves on their own land. Graves were quite shallow, and covered with a stone slab. This was whitewashed to remind people not to walk on it.

TOMBS

Some people were buried in caves, and rich families had tombs cut in rock. All the members of a family would be buried in the same tomb.

The entrance was small and low, and closed off with a large stone which was rolled into place. Inside, passages and stone stairs led from one cave to another. Each cave had stone ledges, or alcoves cut into the wall, where the bodies were placed. In some underground tombs, each small cave had its own door.

When a body had rotted away, the bones were put in a stone box called an ossuary, and placed in an alcove.

AFTER THE FUNERAL

There was a funeral meal, and up to thirty days of mourning. No work was done for the first three days. Very religious people didn't wash during this time.

DIGGING UP THE PAST

Archaeology is the science of studying the remains of earlier times. By digging down into the remains of old cities, we can find out about the people who lived there. People made their settlements by water, and the same site often continued to be used for thousands of years. Gradually, layers of buildings and objects, called strata, built up on top of each other.

A dig

STRATA

Strata tell archaeologists about different periods; for example a layer of ash shows that a city burned down.

Each layer will contain the foundations of buildings, perhaps part of a wall, and sometimes also pottery, jewellery, idols, coins, tools, and weapons. These are all mixed up with soil and rocks. There will be no clothing, leather, paper or wood, as these rot away.

When a wall is found, archaeologists look for the floor that goes with it. A floor shows where one layer ends: anything below the floor belongs to another layer.

STARTING A DIG

Sometimes strata build up to form a hill, or tell. This is often a promising site for digging.

First, a section is dug downwards, to find a good place to start. Then a trench may be dug in steps along the sloping side of the tell. The different strata show up like layers in a cake.

The site is divided into fields measuring 6 sq m (65 sq ft). Each field is divided into even smaller squares. In this way, a plan can be drawn of the site, and each object is marked down exactly where it is found.

A FIND

Groups of archaeologists work in teams in different places on the site. Sieves are used to make sure no tiny objects are missed.

Every single thing found in a square is carefully cleaned, photographed, drawn, described, labelled and put in a bag. Items are then taken away to a museum for further study.

Sieving earth

FAMILIES IN BIBLE TIMES

In the Book of Genesis, Laban said to his nephew Jacob, 'You are my own flesh and blood.' Even distant relatives were regarded as equally part of the whole family (or 'clan'). If one person was in trouble, the others came to help. Nothing was more important than your family.

HUSBANDS

A man was the head of the family. His wife called him 'Master'. A man could have more than one wife, especially if his first wife had no children. But most men could not afford more than two wives.

In New Testament times, it was not common to have more than one wife.

WIVES

In Bible times, a wife was the property of her husband. (Today, most people think this is wrong: a wife is not the property of her husband, but an equal partner in the marriage.) But she was loved and respected by her husband, and she was responsible for creating a happy home for her family.

Bible Search
- Laban to Jacob:
  Genesis 29:14
- Two wives:
  I Samuel 1:1–8
- Peter's mother-in-law:
  Mark 1:29–31

A husband with two wives and children

DIVORCE

Divorce was not approved of, and was probably not very common. To divorce his wife, a man had only to write a letter and give it her. He had to return her dowry (the money or property brought by a woman to her husband when she married).

Divorce

RELIGION IN THE FAMILY

One of the chief religious festivals of the year, the Passover, took place at home with the family, not in the synagogue.

On his thirteenth birthday, a boy was considered to be a man. A religious service called Bar Mitzvah was held in the synagogue, followed by a party. The boy now had to obey the religious laws.

OLD PEOPLE

There were no old people's homes, and elderly people were always looked after by their children. The Gospels tell us that Peter's mother-in-law lived with him.

Old people lived with their family

Waiting for the rain

Bible Search

- A sowing story:
Matthew 13:1–9
- A harvest story:
Matthew 13:24–30
- Harvest festival:
Exodus 23:16

FARMERS
AND GRAIN CROPS

When the Israelites settled in Canaan, they became farmers. Each family was given their own plot of land. All work was done by hand, with the help of working animals.

Farmers waited for the October rains to soften up the rock-hard earth, before starting to plough.

SOWING THE SEED

Fields were ploughed with a simple plough (a stick with a fork at one end) pulled by an ox. Then the farmer walked up and down, throwing handfuls of seed from a basket into the furrows. Next, the field was ploughed again to bury the seed.

A farmer ploughing

HARVESTING

Harvesting

Harvesting started in April, after the March rains. Most farmers used a semi-circular sickle to cut the crops. The crops were tied into sheaves, and loaded on to a cart. A donkey pulled the cart to a level piece of ground known as a threshing floor.

THRESHING

The crops had to be threshed to separate the grain from the stalks. To do this, farmers beat the sheaves with sticks, or an ox trampled over them. Another way of threshing was for an ox to pull a flat, wooden threshing-sledge over the sheaves; the underside of the sledge was studded with stones or iron.

Threshing

WINNOWING

The grain had to be collected from amongst the broken stalks. In the evening, when a breeze sprang up, the threshed corn was tossed into the air with a long-handled wooden winnowing fork. The grain fell to the ground, but the stalks, or chaff, were lighter and blew away in the breeze. Stalks were collected to burn on fires.

GRAIN

The grain was sieved to get rid of bits of stick and stone, and put into sacks to be sold or stored. Flour was made by grinding the grain between two flat stones.

FESTIVALS

A festival, or feast, was held to remember God's goodness, or to ask for his help, or perhaps to renew the promise to serve him. All public holidays were religious festivals. Everyone enjoyed festivals, and often there was a party. The main festivals are described below.

Celebrating Purim

PASSOVER

Passover, in March or April, celebrated the time that the Israelite families escaped the plague which killed the eldest son in every Egyptian family. This was during the time the Israelites were slaves in Egypt.

On the first evening of Passover, a meal of roast lamb and bitter herbs, with unleavened bread (bread made without yeast), was eaten. Unleavened bread was eaten all the following week.

WEEKS

Weeks, later called Pentecost, was the main harvest festival. It was held fifty days after Passover, in June, when the grain harvest had been collected in.

Shelters

DAY OF ATONEMENT

The Day of Atonement was held near the end of September. On this day, no one ate any food. The people asked God to forgive them for their sins. At the Temple, a goat was killed, and a second goat was driven into the desert. This was to show that God had taken away the sins of the people.

SHELTERS OR INGATHERING

In the autumn, a seven-day party was held to celebrate the end of the olive and grape harvests. The people made shelters out of branches, where they slept in memory of the years the Israelites spent in the wilderness after escaping from Egypt. Prayers were held for rain for the new crops.

PURIM

Feasting, drinking, games and fancy-dress parades were held to celebrate the day when God saved the people from their enemies.

DEDICATION

The festival of Dedication, or Lights, took place in December. Each evening, lamps were lit in houses and synagogues to mark the year 165 BC, when the Temple was rebuilt.

Bible Search

- Festivals: *Leviticus 23*
- Day of Atonement: *Leviticus 16*
- Purim: *Esther 3; 9*
- Shelters: *John 7:37–38*
- Dedication: *John 10:22*

FISHING,
FISH AND FISHERMEN

Most fishing in Palestine was done in the Sea of Galilee, which was a large inland lake. On a calm day, over three hundred fishing boats might have fished for the twenty or so different kinds of fish that lived there. At least seven of Jesus' twelve apostles were fishermen.

Bible Search

● A coin:
Matthew 17:24–27

● Jesus preaches from a fishing boat:
Matthew 13:1–23

● Fish for lunch:
John 9:9

MONEY FISH

When Jesus had to pay his Temple tax, he told Peter to go fishing! The first fish Peter caught was holding a silver coin.
(There is a type of fish which carries its young in its mouth. When the young are old enough to look after themselves, the mother picks up an object to stop them gliding back into her mouth. She usually chooses something brightly coloured or shiny.)

FISH TO EAT

Jews did not eat much meat, so fish was a very important everyday food. Fish from the Sea of Galilee was salted, pickled or dried. It was also sold to many other countries.

FISHING BOATS

The fishing boats on the Sea of Galilee were wide, solid and slow. Usually, they had a crew of about six. Often, fishermen clubbed together to buy a boat and some nets. The boats had oars and probably one central sail in the shape of a triangle.

Fishing was very tiring work. Fishermen had to be strong. They had various ways to try and catch fish:
● A line with a bone hook on the end.
● Spearing fish with harpoons.
● Attracting fish to the surface at night with a light.
● Pulling a large drag-net behind a boat.
● Using a throwing-net.

A throwing-net's catch

Spearing fish

THROWING-NETS

When Jesus called Peter and Andrew to follow him, they were 'casting their nets' in the water. These circular nets had weights round the edges. They were thrown over shoals of fish in shallow water. As the net sank, the fish were trapped.

19

FLOWERS,
HERBS AND SPICES

A garlic bulb

I n the Bible, just as all small birds were called 'sparrow' or 'chatterer', so many flowers were called 'lilies'. Flowers were not grown in gardens, so the flowers we read about were wild flowers.

Jesus said, 'See how the lilies of the field grow. They do not labour or spin, yet I tell you that not even Solomon in all his splendour was dressed like one of these.'

Lilies

FLOWERS

In spring and summer, the hills and valleys of Galilee were bright with wild flowers: blue anemones, purple pea blossom, scarlet tulips, yellow narcissi and irises, red poppies and anemones, white daisies and lilies, and different coloured crocuses and hyacinths.

A valley in Gallilee

HERBS AND SPICES

Herbs and spices were used to stop food going bad, to make it taste better, and as a perfume for the body or the air.

The herbs that were used in Bible times are still used today. They include cumin, dill, mint, coriander, cinnamon, rue and saffron.

Myrrh

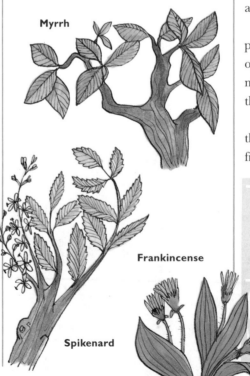

Frankincense

Spikenard

Garlic was common in Egypt and was used to flavour bread. When the Israelites were in the wilderness, after escaping from Egypt, they longed for the garlic of Egypt.

Myrrh was a sweet-smelling resin collected from the branches of a small thorny tree that grew in Arabia and Africa. It was used to make medicine and an oil. Myrrh was put on Jesus' body when he died.

Frankincense was a whitish gum, collected from cuts made in branches of a large tree that grew in Arabia and Africa. It was burned to make a scented smoke. It was very expensive. The wise men who visited the baby Jesus, brought him gifts of frankincense and myrrh.

Gall was a name used for the poisonous hemlock plant or pain-killing opium plant. Jesus was offered wine mixed with gall when he was dying on the cross.

Spikenard was a small spiky plant that grew in India. Oil (nard) collected from the spikes was used as a perfume.

Bible Search

- Solomon and wild flowers: *Luke 12:27–28*
- Spikenard: *John 12:1–8*

FOOD AND COOKING

Corn is being roasted on this metal plate. Sometimes corn is ground and mixed with water to make a porridge.

Jewish laws included certain rules that had to be followed when cooking. For example, meat and milk dishes could not be cooked or eaten together.

On special occasions, such as a wedding, or when a baby was born, there would be a party. Parties went on for many hours, or even days. All sorts of special food would be prepared for a party.

Wine is kept in tall bottles or animal skins, and drunk out of metal cups. Wide cups made of metal, or flat hard rounds of bread, are used for plates.

Grinding grain between two stones to make flour.

Often, the only seasoning used is salt. Sometimes herbs and spices are added too.

To make bread, water is poured into some flour and mixed. Then yeast, or uncooked bread dough left over from the last batch, is added and mixed well. The dough is left to rise, then formed into round shapes. Some dough is put aside for the next day. The bread is baked in an oven, or on an upturned pot over the fire.

Goats' milk is mixed with salt, and left to harden into cheese. It's delicious with fresh bread.

Locusts boiled in salt water have a shrimp-like taste.

Flat pieces of dough are pressed on the inside of a chimney-shaped oven, and left to cook.

Cakes are made with wheat flour, mixed with water and sweetened with honey. Eggs are not used. Cakes may be flavoured with mint or cinnamon. Honey doughnuts are made into animal shapes and fried in olive oil.

Grasshoppers are often fried in olive oil.

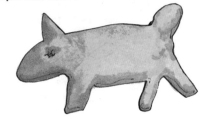

Food is cooked on fires outside, or near the door in the living room. Only large houses have kitchens. A lamb and a calf have been killed, and are being roasted on a spit.

Turkish delight is made from starch (from corn), mixed with honey, and with pistachio nuts or almonds added.

To make locust biscuits, locusts are dried in the sun, ground into a paste, mixed with honey and wheat flour, and baked over a fire.

This boy is hungry. He's dipped a piece of bread in honey.

This skin bag, hung between three sticks, contains goat's milk. It's shaken and squeezed until butter is formed.

21

FOOD AND DRINK

Making a stew

Jewish meals were fairly simple. Bread was the main food. There were usually two meals a day, but not at set times. People ate when they were hungry. The evening meal was the only time the family sat down together to eat (apart from on the Sabbath).

BREAD

Poor people ate bread made from barley, and rich people ate bread made from wheat. It was shaped into round, flat buns. It quickly went dry and mouldy, and fresh bread had to be baked every two or three days. Bread was broken and not cut.

VEGETABLES AND PULSES

Leek

A soup made of vegetables and sometimes pulses (peas, beans, lentils), was eaten every evening with bread. Lentils, beans, onions, garlic, and leeks were all common. There were no potatoes, carrots, parsnips or cabbage. People also ate lettuce, chicory and cucumber.

Garlic

Pulses

Lettuce

FRUIT

Figs, grapes, apricots and dates were eaten fresh from the tree. These fruits were also dried and pressed together to make 'cakes'. Olives were pickled or eaten fresh. People also enjoyed other fruits, such as pomegranates and melons, and nuts such as pistachios, walnuts and almonds. There may have been apples, but there were no oranges or bananas.

Bible Search

- A boy's lunch: *John 6:8*
- Esau's meal: *Genesis 25:34*
- Breakfast: *John 21:9*
- Emergency rations: *2 Samuel 17:28–29*

MEAT AND FISH

Meat was a luxury. If a guest was expected, mutton, lamb or goat might be added to the evening stew. Roast meat was a great treat. Jewish laws said that only meat from animals which ate grass and had cloven hoofs could be eaten. Pork was forbidden.

Neither chicken nor eggs were eaten in Palestine.

Fish was an important everyday food, which was salted or dried. Jewish laws only allowed fish with scales and fins to be eaten.

DRINKS

People drank milk, but it was usually goat's milk, rather than cow's milk. Yogurt drinks were also made from milk. Grapes and pomegranates were boiled down to make a rich, sweet drink. Grape juice and red wine were very popular.

HONEY

Cane sugar was not known, so honey was very important for sweetening food. For children, it was a great treat to be given part of a honeycomb to eat.

FURNITURE IN RICH AND POOR HOMES

I f we looked into a typical house in Palestine in Jesus' time, we would think that it was almost empty, because there would be so little furniture.

When the Israelites lived as nomads in tents in the desert, their furniture had to be easy to pack and carry on camels or donkeys. So people only owned basic, essential items. Things did not change greatly later on, when the Israelites settled down and lived in houses.

Nomads carried their furniture on camels

TABLES AND CHAIRS

Poor people ate on the floor

Rich people's houses often had very low benches running along two or three sides of the room. Sometimes these were covered with beautiful cushions.

Poor people didn't have any chairs. The only type of seat would have been a stool, but most people sat on mats on the floor.

An animal skin spread out on the floor was used as a table.

ROMAN SEATING

The Romans used dining couches when they ate. These couches were arranged in a horseshoe shape around a table. Servants came through the gap to bring the food. The guests lay stretched out on the couches, while they enjoyed their meal.

The Romans ate while lying on couches

BEDS

The poorer you were, the closer you slept to the ground! Kings and wealthy people slept in bronze or wooden beds with legs.

Most people slept on the floor on mats. These were sometimes stuffed with wool. There were no blankets. People wrapped themselves in their cloaks or covered themselves with a goatskin. If you were lucky, you might have a stuffed goatskin for a pillow. More often, people had wooden, or even stone pillows. Babies slept in woollen cradles slung from the roof, or sometimes even in an animal's feeding trough, as Jesus did.

LIGHT AND STORAGE

Food and clothes were stored in wooden chests.

Lamps would be placed on a metal lampstand, or in a hollow in the wall. Big earthenware pots held water. There were pottery jars for flour and olive oil, and bowls for cooking and eating.

Bible Search

- A stone pillow:
  Genesis 28:11

- Rich living:
  Amos 6:4

- Luxury bedroom furniture:
  2 Kings 4:10

GARDENS
IN CITIES AND VILLAGES

In cities, houses were crowded together. Only very rich people could afford gardens. Their big houses had courtyards with fountains, ornamental pools and flowering trees. Sometimes they had gardens outside the city walls. These were often shady orchards. In villages, some people had gardens by their houses. But water was limited, and gardening was work. Vegetables and herbs were grown to eat and sell in the markets.

THE KING OF PERSIA

The Book of Esther describes the king's garden at his palace in Susa. There were white and blue drapes, tied with white and purple cords to silver rings on marble pillars. The floor was made from marble, inlaid with mother-of-pearl, shells and jewels.

Bible Search

- A bride: *Song of Songs 4:12*
- Ahab's greed: *1 Kings 21*
- A king's garden: *Esther 1:5–6*
- Gethsemene: *Mark 14:32–42*

KING AHAB'S GREED

King Ahab wanted to buy Naboth's vineyard, but Naboth refused to sell it. King Ahab's wife, Jezebel, didn't understand Ahab's problem. In her view, the people and the land all belonged to the king. She arranged for Naboth to be stoned to death. Then she took over his vineyard.

The prophet Elijah told Ahab how wicked he had been, and Ahab was very ashamed and sorry for what he had done. God forgave him, but because Ahab's crime was so serious, God said he would punish Ahab's descendants.

GARDEN OF GETHSEMENE

Jesus often went to the Garden of Gethsemene outside Jerusalem. The word 'Gethsemene' means 'olive press'. The garden was a grove of olive trees. It was one of many private gardens on the slopes of the Mount of Olives. Here, Jesus could escape from the crowds. It was here that he spent his last night.

A TOMB IN THE GARDEN

Wealthy people were sometimes buried in caves in the hillside. Often, a garden was planted in front of the tomb. Jesus was buried in a garden tomb like this. When Mary first saw Jesus, after he had risen from the dead, she thought he was the gardener.

A king's garden

GOVERNMENT
IN OLD TESTAMENT TIMES

The Jewish nation grew from the descendants of one man: Abraham. Abraham's grandson, Jacob, had twelve sons. Their families became the twelve clans, or tribes, of Israel. Jacob, his sons and their families, went to live in Egypt to escape famine in Canaan. Over many years, their numbers grew. In Egypt we first hear of 'elders', who were leaders among the Israelite people.

MOSES

Hundreds of years later, the Egyptian rulers made the Israelites into slaves. But eventually Moses, one of the Israelite leaders, led the slaves out of Egypt. To deal with arguments and difficulties, he split the people into groups, led by elders.

An Egyptian ruler

JUDGES

Joshua took over from Moses. When the Israelites reached the Promised Land, he divided it into twelve areas, one for each tribal group. There was no central government. A judge, who was rather like a cross between a sherrif, a warrior chief and a preacher, ruled over one tribe or group of tribes. In each village, elders led the people.

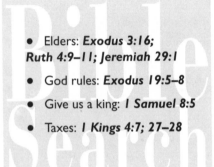

Bible Search

- Elders: *Exodus 3:16; Ruth 4:9–11; Jeremiah 29:1*
- God rules: *Exodus 19:5–8*
- Give us a king: *I Samuel 8:5*
- Taxes: *I Kings 4:7; 27–28*

The kingdoms of the twelve tribes of Israel

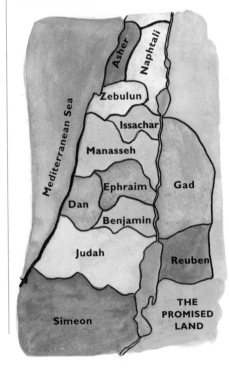

Asher
Naphtali
Zebulun
Issachar
Manasseh
Mediterranean Sea
Ephraim
Gad
Dan
Benjamin
Judah
Reuben
Simeon
THE PROMISED LAND

KINGS

As time went on, the Israelites felt they wanted a king. God chose Saul to be the first king; he was followed by David.

David had a full-time army, and needed money to pay for it. That meant that people had to start paying taxes.

Money to pay taxes

When David's son Solomon became king, he divided the country into twelve districts with a governor in charge of collecting taxes in each district. Solomon ruled from Jerusalem with the help of a full-time staff. Each village had its own council of elders.

OCCUPYING ARMIES

When the country was invaded by foreign armies, the Israelites were ruled by governors chosen by the invaders.

Under Greek rule, a Council of Jewish elders, led by the High Priest, was in charge of religious affairs. In 143 BC, the people broke free from Greek rule. The High Priest now ruled the country. This lasted until the Romans captured Jerusalem in 63 BC.

The High Priest

GOVERNMENT
IN NEW TESTAMENT TIMES

A Roman coin

There was civil war, yet again, in Palestine. Many Jews were sick of the fighting. In 63 BC, the Romans stepped in to bring some peace and order to the land. That was the start of the Roman occupation.

In 37 BC, the Romans put the half-Jewish Herod in power.

KING HEROD THE GREAT

In many ways, Herod was a clever ruler. The golden and ivory Temple in Jerusalem was built on his orders.

But the Jews hated Herod, and he was so terrified of losing his throne that he turned into a crazed killer. When news reached Herod that a baby had been born in Bethlehem who would become king of the Jews, he ordered all baby boys in Bethlehem to be put to death.

Herod orders the killing of baby boys

HEROD'S SONS

When Herod died, the Romans divided the country into three, and put three of his sons in charge: Archelaus, Herod Antipas, and Philip.

Archelaus was made ruler of Judea and Samaria in the south. He was cruel and stupid. After ten years, the Jews begged the Romans to get rid of him. Then Judea was made a Roman province and a Roman governor, called a procurator, was put in charge. Pontius Pilate was procurator during Jesus' time.

Herod Antipas was made ruler of Galilee. The third son, Philip, ruled Iturea in the far north-east. He was a gentle and clever man.

THE SANHEDRIN

The Sanhedrin

As long as the Jews paid the Roman taxes, and didn't rebel, the Romans allowed them to rule themselves. A council of religious leaders, called the Sanhedrin, was made up of seventy specially chosen men. They were priests, teachers of the law, elders (men from the most important families), Sadducees and Pharisees (the two opposing religious parties). The High Priest was in charge. The Sanhedrin had the power to judge, punish and imprison people brought before it.

HOBBIES AND GAMES

The prophet Zechariah wrote that the 'city streets will be filled with boys and girls playing there'. Bible writers did not describe the games children played. Instead, we learn about them from objects found by archaeologists, and from paintings on pottery and walls.

Bible Search

- Samson's riddle: *Judges 14:10–20*
- Children's games: *Matthew 11:16–17*
- Throwing dice: *Mark 15:24*

HOBBIES

People probably didn't have hobbies. The sort of things we may have as hobbies, such as craftwork, or fishing, were skills that people put to good use to earn money. There were no bird-watchers or chariot-spotters!

GAMES

Jesus talked of children playing at weddings and funerals. The prophet Isaiah said, 'Little ones dance about. They sing to the music of tambourine and harp.'

We know that Roman children played ball games. For one game, everyone stood in a circle and threw a ball from one person to another. The winner was the person who dropped the ball least often.

Roman girls would play knucklebones, which was the same as our game of jacks or fives.

In many places, archaeologists have found squares scratched on the pavements, as if for hopscotch. Riddles and quizzes were popular at parties, and sometimes prizes were given.

TOYS

Archaeologists have found rattles and whistles, and also tiny clay pots and furniture. Little figures have also been found, but these may be idols, not dolls. Jewish children probably did not play with dolls, as the Jewish law did not allow people to make images of people.

Many playing boards for board games have been found, made out of wood, clay or even ivory. These were for chess, solitaire, ludo, and draughts.

DICE

Dice have also been discovered. Soldiers threw dice to decide who would get Jesus' cloak when he was killed. They probably carried dice around with them in their belts.

Dice were thrown and pieces of wood moved into squares, where they were robed, crowned or given a sceptre. This may be the game scratched on the floor of the Antonia Fortress in Jerusalem. Perhaps soldiers played this game on the night Jesus was caught, and used Jesus as the playing piece.

Jewish law forbade gambling.

HOMES CAVES
AND EARLY HOUSES

The earliest homes, in the Stone Age, were caves. Caves gave shelter from wind and rain, and protection from wild animals. By the time the Bible was written, some people still lived in caves.

The first houses looked rather like caves, and were built out of stone.

CAVES

Very poor people, who could not afford houses, lived in caves. And caves were a good place to live and hide for people who were on the run from their enemies. A cave was the headquarters and home of David and his outlaws, when he was hiding from Saul.

Caves also made good hideouts for gangs of robbers.

A home in a cave

WHAT WERE CAVE HOMES LIKE?

A natural cave could be made bigger with flint tools. Seats were cut out of stone, and a hollow might be made in the wall, where a lamp could be placed. Walls were sometimes decorated. A hearth would be made near the mouth of the cave, so that smoke from the fire could escape.

The family lived near the entrance of the cave, where it was lighter. Food would be stored at the back of the cave, or in a smaller cave leading off the main cave.

STABLES

Sometimes caves were turned into stables for animals. The story of Jesus' birth tells us he was born in a stable: this may have been a cave.

VERY EARLY HOUSES

By about 4000 BC, New Stone Age men had left their caves. Some learned to be farmers. They built small, round, cave-like homes out of stone. Their houses were grouped close together for safety, and surrounded by a stone wall. Traces of these first houses have been found in Jericho, which is probably the oldest city in the world, founded about 8000 BC.

Bible Search

- Israelites in caves: *Judges 6:2*
- David in hiding: *1 Samuel 22:1*
- Homes for poor people: *Hebrews 11:38*

HOMES LIVING IN TENTS

Donkeys carried the bags

People who lived a travelling life were called nomads. They moved from one water-hole to another with their flocks. They lived in tents.

Abraham, Isaac and Jacob all lived in tents. Their descendants, the Israelites, never forgot that they came from wandering tent dwellers.

Seats were carpets or straw mats, and beds were mats. The table was a round piece of leather. It had rings round the edge so that a cord could be threaded through and drawn up into a bag to use when travelling. Water-bottles were made from goat's skin. There were baskets for storage, and the few cooking pots were made out of metal.

WHAT WERE TENTS MADE OF?

At first, tents were made from animal skins. Later, when people learned how to weave, they were made from goat or camel hair.

The skins were held up by wooden poles measuring up to 2 m (7 ft) high. The more important you were, the more poles you had. Usually there were nine. The centre pole was slightly taller than the rest. Wooden pegs and ropes kept the tent steady. The tent's entrance faced the direction from which visitors were most likely to come, and was kept open during the day. This was so it looked welcoming.

Animal skin

Rope and pegs

Tent poles

Richer families might have a group of tents, with separate tents for the women and children, and for servants. The main tent was put up in the middle with the servants' tents surrounding it.

INSIDE A TENT

Inside were two rooms divided by a curtain. The back room was for women and children, and was where the cooking was done. There was very little furniture, because everything had to be carried on donkeys when people moved on to their next camp.

SETTING UP CAMP

Campsites were set up near water, and close to trees which could give shelter. There was always a danger from wild animals, and from other nomads too. Sometimes there were fights over wells and the use of precious water.

- Quarrels over water: *Genesis 26:19–22*

- Abraham's tent: *Genesis 18:1–2*

29

HOMES VILLAGE HOUSES

T he simplest village houses were like a square box, with a flat roof. The whole family and their animals slept in one room. Other houses had a wall outside, enclosing a yard, where the animals could be kept. Richer families might have an extra storey.

Bible Search

- Roof of clay and branches on wooden beams: *Mark 2:4*
- Safety first: *Deuteronomy 28:8*
- Extra bedroom: *2 Kings 4:10*

UP ON THE ROOF

Houses had a flat roof with a slight curve to allow rain to flow into a gutter. There was a low wall round the roof to stop people falling off.

The roof was used like an extra room. Grapes and figs were spread out to dry along with wet clothes. People would go out there to pray and think. They sat out talking to their friends, or even held parties there. On warm nights, the family slept on the roof.

WALLS

Walls were made of stone (in rocky areas), or built from mud and straw bricks which had been baked in an oven. Bricks were stuck together by a mortar made from lime. Foundations were important because Palestine was in an earthquake area. If a house was not built on rock, foundations were dug to be as deep as the walls were high.

Walls were often whitewashed.

WINDOWS AND DOORS

There were only one or two small high windows, with no glass. In winter, these might be covered by an animal skin.

Small windows kept the house cool in summer and warmer in winter.

The doorposts were made of wood or stone. Doors were only closed at night, or when there was no one at home. Doorways were low, and grown-ups had to stoop to go in.

INSIDE A HOUSE

Inside the house was a raised platform made from stone, or mud and stone chippings, where the family lived. Next to it was a floor of stamped-down earth, where the animals slept at night. There was a manger for the animals' food. People lived outdoors and on the roof as much as possible. Food and pots were stored in a hollow in the wall.

A fire would be lit in a hollow. There was no chimney, and the room was smoky when the fire was lit. The walls were black from smoke. Lots of insects lived in cracks and holes in the walls. There was a store area where food for winter and tools were kept. Houses were only about 1.8 m (6 ft) high.

HOMES TOWN HOUSES

T he people of Israel were not especially good builders or architects, but the house design below seems have been invented by them, and was common. This type of house would have been lived in by a family with an average income.

In Jerusalem, archaeologists have found the remains of a town house that was burnt down by the Romans in AD 70. It had a basement with a kitchen, bathroom, courtyard and three other small rooms. There were about twenty rooms on the ground floor, and another floor as well. There were large stone basins for storing water.

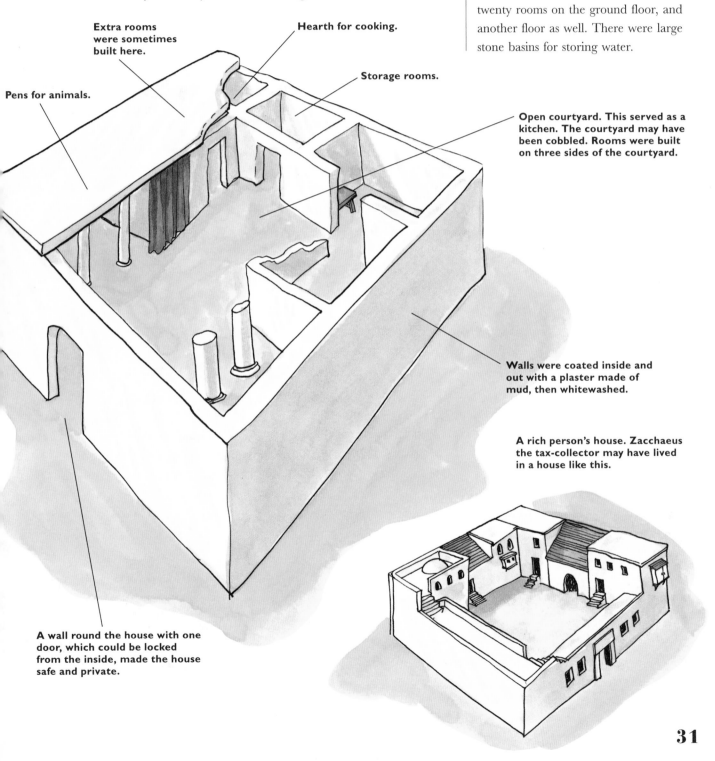

Extra rooms were sometimes built here.

Hearth for cooking.

Storage rooms.

Pens for animals.

Open courtyard. This served as a kitchen. The courtyard may have been cobbled. Rooms were built on three sides of the courtyard.

Walls were coated inside and out with a plaster made of mud, then whitewashed.

A rich person's house. Zacchaeus the tax-collector may have lived in a house like this.

A wall round the house with one door, which could be locked from the inside, made the house safe and private.

Fetching water

HOUSEWORK — A DAY IN A VILLAGE HOME

The mother was in charge of the home. The Book of Proverbs shows how important she was and how much she had to do: weaving wool and flax, providing food, buying land, and making clothes for her family.

GETTING UP

The family was woken by the crowing of a cockerel at dawn. Cockerels were the first alarm clocks! The smallest houses only had one room, with a raised area where people slept and ate. When everyone got up, the flat mattresses which were their beds were rolled up.

People didn't sit down to breakfast. Instead, bread and dried fruit or cheese was eaten on the move.

Then the father and the older boys set off for work. Younger children stayed at home. Some learned about God, and how to read and write, from priests or other religious leaders.

CHORES

The younger children looked after the animals. Many people kept sheep and goats. At night, the animals were kept in the lower part of the room, next to the raised area. Older girls were often sent to fetch water from the well. Most villages were on a hill, and most wells were at the bottom of the hill!

There was little or no furniture to dust. The earth floor was swept with a broom made from corn stalks tied to a stick.

SHOPPING

Food did not keep well in the hot climate. Vegetables and fruit had to be bought fresh from the market. Grain was ground into flour to make bread, or bread could be bought from the baker. Grain was ground between two stones. Poor families used barley, and rich families used wheat.

IN THE AFTERNOON

During the middle of the day, which was the hottest part, everyone slept. Then, in the afternoon, clothes were made and mended, or washed in the river and spread out to dry on the flat roof. Other jobs to do were weaving and spinning, and preparing the evening meal. The women and girls worked outside in the shade.

THE EVENING MEAL

The family often sat outside to eat. There might be a big pot of soup, and everyone would dip pieces of bread in it. This meant no washing up! When it got dark, the family went to bed.

Making the bed

IDOLS
WORSHIPPING FALSE GODS

A n idol was an object, like a statue, which represented a god. People worshipped the image as a god. It may seem strange that anyone should want to bow down and worship a lump of metal or wood. But in the times before their exile to Babylonia, the Israelites were often tempted to copy their neighbours and worship idols instead of God.

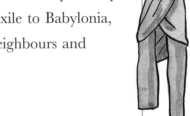

THE GOLDEN CALF

The Israelites were waiting for Moses to come down from Mount Sinai, where he had gone to talk to God. Moses was gone for a long time, and nobody knew what had happened to him. So the people asked Aaron to make them a new god. They gave him all their gold jewellery, and Aaron made it into a gleaming idol in the shape of a calf. The people began to pray and offer sacrifices to it.

In Egypt (which the Israelites had recently left), a bull stood for fertility and power.

Worshipping the golden calf

FORBIDDEN

Moses said to the Israelites, 'You saw no form of any kind the day the Lord spoke to you at Horeb (Sinai). Therefore…do not make for yourselves an idol, an image of any shape…'

Other nations believed in gods which looked like people or animals. They made idols of their gods, and sometimes worshipped these idols.

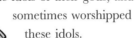

GODS

Baal was the god of storms and war. He was the most important of the gods of the people of Canaan.

Astarte, or Ashtaroth, was a mother goddess, a goddess of fertility, love and war.

Astarte was a mother goddess

Baal was the god of storms and war

Teraphim were sometimes called 'household gods'. They were small images of human figures used in worship and magic, and for getting in touch with evil powers.

A teraph

EVIL

In New Testament times, Greeks and Romans sometimes worshipped idols. Paul said that while idols were not real, people who worshipped them could be trapped by evil spirits.
See also the page on Worship.

Bible Search

- Moses: *Deuteronomy 4:15–16*
- Isaiah makes fun of idols: *Isaiah 44:9–20*
- Teraphim: *2 Kings 23:24*
- Paul: *1 Corinthians 10:19–20*

ILLNESS
AND MEDICINE

I llnesses such as dysentery, cholera, typhoid and beriberi were common. Skin diseases, especially leprosy, affected many people. (See the page on Beggars and Lepers.) People often suffered from worms. Many children had an eye infection called ophthalmia, which was passed on by flies.

Many children had ophthalmia

- Wine for the stomach: *1 Timothy 5:23*
- Oil and wine for a wound: *Luke 10:34*
- Wine and myrrh for Jesus: *Mark 15:23*
- A sick woman: *Mark 5:25–29; Luke 8:43*

- Honey was used as an ointment for open wounds.
- Wine was drunk for stomach disorders.
- Wine mixed with a drug called myrrh made a simple pain-killing drink. Jesus was offered this drink when he was dying on the cross.

Wine and myrrh was used as a pain-killer

- Figs were used to cure boils. When King Hezekiah had a bad boil, Isaiah made a hot paste from figs to put on it.

DOCTORS

In Old Testament times, there were not many doctors. The Egyptians tried to cure illnesses by magic spells. The Israelites thought of health as a gift from God, and asked for God's help when they became ill.

By the time of the New Testament, there were many more doctors. Jewish religious teachers said no one should live in a town without a doctor.

A woman came to Jesus to be cured. Mark and Luke both wrote about it in their Gospels. Mark said, 'She had suffered a great deal under the care of many doctors, and spent all she had…' But Luke, who was himself a doctor, was kinder to doctors! He wrote: 'No one could heal her.'

MEDICINES

People used all sorts of things, such as herbs, as medicines:

- Olive oil mixed with herbs could be used to bathe the head of a sick person.
- A solution of olive oil and wine was put on wounds.

Olive oil was used on wounds

DENTISTS

There were no dentists. Garlic was used for toothache, and yeast was rubbed on painful gums.

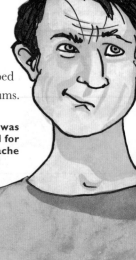

Garlic was used for toothache

34

INSECTS AND REPTILES

Insects are the largest group of animals in the world, with over a million species. Ants, bees, flies, gnats, grasshoppers and moths all have walk-on parts in the Bible story.

Reptiles are animals with scales instead of fur, skin or hide. Only lizards and snakes appear in the Bible.

LOCUSTS

Locusts are a kind of grasshopper. They can destroy crops.

People ate locusts because they were a good source of fat and protein. You could have boiled locust, roasted locust or even locust cake. John the Baptist ate locusts with honey, which helped to take away their bitter flavour.

BEES

Sugar was not known, so honey was used to sweeten food. People did not have beehives, but they did put up hanging baskets or pots, hoping that bees would nest there.

Locusts eating crops

Ants

Bible Search

- Harvester ant: **Proverbs 6:6-7**
- Wicked people and snakes: **Psalm 58:4-5**
- Paul on Malta: **Acts 28:1-6**
- Jonathan finds honey: **I Samuel 14:24-28**

SNAKES

In the Garden of Eden, the Devil made himself look like a snake, so snakes were thought of as evil. The Old Testament has eight different words which all mean 'poisonous snake'. Different translations describe snakes as adders, asps, cobras, serpents and vipers. The New Testament Greek word for all snakes is viper. Snake charmers appear once in the Bible. A psalmist says that evil people who refuse to listen to God are rather like snakes that refuse to listen to the snake charmer's pipe.

Snake charmer

PAUL AND THE VIPER

Paul was shipwrecked on Malta. While collecting sticks for a fire, Paul was bitten by a viper. The islanders expected the poison would kill him, but nothing happened. They were amazed and decided Paul must be a god.

Viper

35

JERUSALEM
IN THE TIME OF JESUS

I t is about 3,000 years since King David captured the small hilltop town of Jerusalem and made it his capital city. David's son, King Solomon, built the Temple in Jerusalem, making it a holy city. Nearly a thousand years later, King Herod rebuilt the Temple. Then, as now, tourists from all over the world came to Jerusalem.

ANY QUESTIONS
1 Who founded the city of Jerusalem?
2 Where did the Devil tempt Jesus?

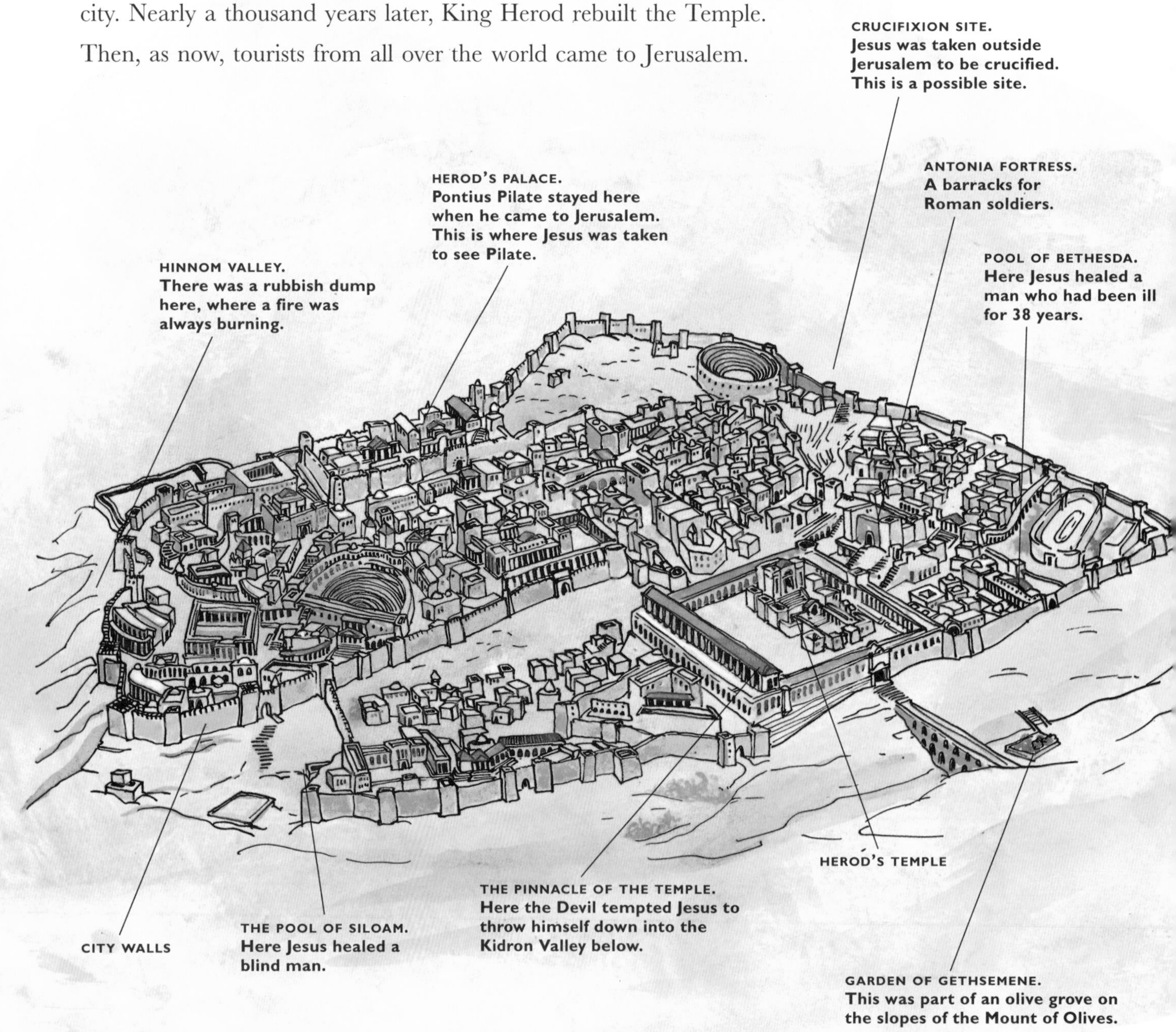

CRUCIFIXION SITE.
Jesus was taken outside Jerusalem to be crucified. This is a possible site.

ANTONIA FORTRESS.
A barracks for Roman soldiers.

HEROD'S PALACE.
Pontius Pilate stayed here when he came to Jerusalem. This is where Jesus was taken to see Pilate.

POOL OF BETHESDA.
Here Jesus healed a man who had been ill for 38 years.

HINNOM VALLEY.
There was a rubbish dump here, where a fire was always burning.

CITY WALLS

THE POOL OF SILOAM.
Here Jesus healed a blind man.

THE PINNACLE OF THE TEMPLE.
Here the Devil tempted Jesus to throw himself down into the Kidron Valley below.

HEROD'S TEMPLE

GARDEN OF GETHSEMENE.
This was part of an olive grove on the slopes of the Mount of Olives.

JEWELS AND METALS

The Israelites knew six metals: gold, silver, iron, lead, tin and copper. Of these, only iron and copper were found in their country. Gold, silver, tin and lead had to be imported. Precious stones were bought from other countries such as Arabia, Egypt, India, and Africa.

Bible Search

- A smith at work:
Isaiah 44:12

- Any old iron?:
I Samuel 13:19–22

- A chest full of jewels:
Exodus 28:15–29

JEWELS

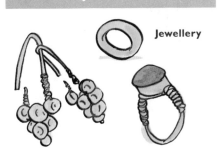

Jewellery

Precious stones were made into smooth shapes and polished. Then they were set in silver, gold or copper to make nose-rings, earrings, rings, bracelets, necklaces, brooches and diadems.

The High Priest wore a breastplate set with twelve beautiful jewels including ruby, topaz, beryl, turquoise, sapphire, emerald, jacinth, agate and amethyst.

The High Priest

SEALS

Seals

Seals were stamped into a plug of soft wax which was put on letters, or sometimes boxes, to keep them private. A broken seal showed that the letter had been opened.

A seal might be made out of a small jewel, cut to an oval shape, polished and then engraved.

Archaeologists have found thousands of seals. Some have pictures of gods or animals. Seals found in Israel are engraved with patterns, plants and names. Often, a hole was drilled through the seal so it could be worn as a necklace or ring.

METALWORKERS

The men who worked iron, copper, silver, gold and lead were very respected craftsmen.

Gold and silversmiths had small furnaces where the metals were melted. Molten gold was poured into moulds. Gold was also hammered into thin sheets and then cut into strips. These were used for embroidery.

COPPER

Three thousand years before the birth of Jesus, people dug copper ore out of the earth. It was heated (in a process called smelting) to extract the copper. A thousand years later, people learned to make bronze by adding tin to copper. Bronze is stronger than copper, but not as strong as iron.

SMITHS

The Israelites only learned to make iron in the time of David. Once it was made iron was beaten out on an anvil to make weapons and tools. It was hard work!

Working with iron

JEWS,
GENTILES, AND
SAMARITANS

A Jew is someone who is descended from Jacob, the grandson of Abraham, or someone whose religion is Judaism. Jews are often called 'the chosen people', because God chose to work with the Jews to save the people of the world. Jesus and the first Christians were Jews.

The Samaritans wanted to help rebuild the Temple

CHANGE OF NAME

Jews were first known as Hebrews, or Israelites, and their country was Israel. (Jacob was given the second name 'Israel' by God.) Later the country split into two: Israel in the north, and Judah in the south. Over three hundred years later, the people of Judah were taken prisoner to Babylonia. After this time they were called Jews, from the word Judah.

GENTILES

Jews call non-Jews 'Gentiles'. In New Testament times, many non-Jews were attracted to the Jewish faith.

JUDAISM

Jews stress the importance of keeping the Old Testament laws. They are waiting for the coming of a great king.

Bible Search

- Samaritan religion: *2 Kings 17:25–34*
- A Samaritan woman: *John 4*
- The Good Samaritan: *Luke 10:25–37*

SAMARITANS

Samaritans take their name from Samaria. When King Solomon died and the country split into two, Samaria became the capital city of the northern kingdom, Israel. Two hundred years later, Israel was invaded by the Assyrians, and large numbers of the people were taken prisoner. The invaders married among the remaining Israelites, and added the worship of God to their own religions.

Old Testament scrolls

When the Jews came back from exile in Babylonia, the Samaritans wanted to help them to rebuild the Temple. But the Jews would not let them.

Samaria was a small area right in the middle of the country. Samaritans and Jews did not like each other. Jews who wanted to travel from Galilee to Jerusalem would usually not go through Samaria. They went a long way round, across the River Jordan.

Taking the long way round

SAMARITAN RELIGION

About 330 years before the birth of Jesus, the Samaritans set up their own temple on Mount Gerizim, with priests and sacrifices. Their Bible was the first five books of the Old Testament.

LANGUAGES
AND WRITING

The earliest writing we know about takes the form of drawings on cave walls. The earliest cave pictures are about 30,000 years old. Pictures, instead of words, were used to describe objects.

Later civilizations also used picture symbols. The ancient Egyptians drew beautiful pictures, which we call hieroglyphics. They had 800 picture symbols.

Hieroglyphics

THE ROSETTA STONE

For a long time, no one could read the hieroglyphics on Egyptian tombs. But in 1798, near the city of Rosetta in Egypt, one of Napoleon's soldiers dug up a large stone with writing all over it. It was a royal command dating from about 200 BC. The command was written in Greek, in everyday Egyptian and in old hieroglyphic Egyptian. At last translators were able break the code and unlock the secrets of ancient Egypt. The stone became known as the Rosetta Stone.

The Rosetta Stone is discovered

CUNEIFORM

The Babylonians used a very simple form of picture writing. They pressed shapes into soft clay with wedge-shaped sticks or bones. The clay was baked in the sun.

These 'books' can still be read today (see the page on Schools).

ALPHABET

In Canaan, in about 1500 BC, a genius invented the alphabet. He or she divided language into twenty simple sounds and wrote down a symbol for each sound. Over the years, each symbol became a letter.

HEBREW

Nearly all our Old Testament was written in Hebrew. Hebrew has twenty-two consonants, but no vowels. It is read from right to left, perhaps because the first Hebrew writing was chiselled on stone. It was easier for most people to chisel from right to left! Hebrew books start from the back.

Chiselling from right to left

GREEK

All our New Testament books are written in Greek. This was the language spoken by the Romans, who ruled most of the world in New Testament times.

ARAMAIC

Small parts of the Old Testament are written in Aramaic. This was the language of the Persian empire, which was the world super-power before the Romans.

Jesus and his disciples spoke Aramaic, and there are a few Aramaic words in the New Testament. 'Abba' is Aramaic for 'father', or 'daddy'.

LETTERS
AND NEWS

Television, faxes and telephones

Many people today are 'news-aholics'. We have TV, radio, newspapers, phones, fax machines and computers to tell each other what is going on in our lives and in the rest of the world. How did people spread news in Bible times?

Computers and radios

CUNEIFORM

Cuneiform writing

The Babylonians wrote letters by pressing a wedge-shaped stick into soft, thin, clay bricks (called tablets). These were left to harden in the sun. This type of writing is called cuneiform. Thousands of cuneiform tablets have been found by archaeologists.

PAPYRUS

The Egyptians made a rough paper from papyrus reeds. Reeds were also used as pens, cut at one end to a sloping point. Black ink was made from soot, olive oil, resin and water.

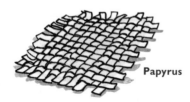

Papyrus

PARCHMENT

The Hebrew word for 'book' comes from the word 'scrape'. Skins of sheep and goats were dried, scraped and softened to make a smooth surface. This was called parchment, and was used for writing on.

ROMANS

The Romans sometimes used two pieces of wood covered with wax for letters. Leather bands held two edges together so that the letter opened like a book. The letter would be written with a bone, bronze or silver stylus. This was pointed at one end, and flat at the other for smoothing the wax.

SENDING LETTERS

A letter might be written on a scroll, which was a long roll of parchment or papyrus. The letter was signed, rolled up, and tied with a cord. Then the knot was covered with wax, and the wax was stamped with a seal. Every man of any importance had his own seal. (See the page on Jewels.)

Bible Search

- Paul signs off: *Galatians 6:11*
- Scrolls and parchments: *2 Timothy 4:13*
- A Roman notice: *John 19:19–22*

POSTAL SERVICE

The first postal service was started by the Persian king, Darius, in about 500 BC. The Romans copied his idea. Letters were taken by messengers on horseback. The messengers rode in relays. Every 24–32 km (15–20 miles), there were rest houses and fresh horses.

Messengers were only used by the Romans and their employees. Other people could hire letter-carriers. These men carried messages in wooden tubes round their neck or waist. Or people sent slaves, or relied on friends, to take messages.

LIGHTING AND HEATING

In the time of Jesus, lamps were kept burning all night. Most houses had only one or two small windows, and so houses were dark. A lamp was often kept lit all day as well. Lamps were very important, and in Bible stories sometimes represented life itself.

Houses didn't have fireplaces or chimneys. A brazier (a container for burning things) might be taken indoors, or a fire would be lit in a hollow in the floor lined with stones. The fuel was animal dung, charcoal or wood.

LAMPS

The earliest lamps were clay dishes, with one end pressed to make a lip. A wick of rush, flax or rag was put in the lip. It soaked up oil contained in the dish. These lamps would burn for two or three hours before they needed to be refilled with oil.

By New Testament times, potters had learned how to make lamps with tops. They were safer because the oil couldn't spill out.

Some lamps had room for several wicks to give more light.

Most lamps burned olive oil, but sometimes animal fat was used. Olive oil was expensive.

Oil jar

TORCHES, CANDLES AND LANTERNS

Outside, in processions, torches were often used. To make a torch, you drenched rags in oil, fastened them to a stick and then lit them. About every fifteen minutes, the charred ends of the rags had to be cut, and more oil added.

Candles were only used in funeral processions, and by the poorest people who could not afford oil for lamps.

To make a lantern, a lamp could be put inside a pottery or metal container. The container had an opening at the side.

Bible Search

- Five silly girls and their lamps: *Matthew 25:1–13*
- What Jesus said about a lamp: *Matthew 5:15–16*
- Lamp means life: *Pslam 18:28*

In one of Jesus' stories, five bridesmaids at a wedding ran out of oil for their lamps

MAKE-UP, HAIRSTYLES, PERFUME, JEWELLERY

A comb

Make-up was popular in all the lands of the Bible. Archaeologists have found hundreds of little cosmetic pots made from ivory, bone and metal. Exquisite jewellery, combs, jewels, ornaments and mirrors have also been discovered.

A cosmetic pot

Bible Search

- Jewels:
  Isaiah: 3:18–23
- A warning:
  1 Peter 3:3–4
- Jezebel:
  2 Kings 9:30

MAKE-UP

Eyes were outlined in black; eyebrows were darkened; eyelids were shaded; eyelashes were thickened with blue colouring. Cheeks were powdered, and rouge was added to lips and cheeks. Women also painted their fingernails and the palms of their hands with a yellowy-orange paste made from henna plant leaves, mixed with oil.

Make-up and jewellery

JEWELLERY

Egyptian jewellery

Egyptians were especially gifted at making jewellery. They would wear wide collar-like necklaces, studded with jewels. Some jewellery was worn as magic charms. A precious stone in the shape of a scarab beetle was said to be a powerful charm.

The Jews liked to wear jewellery: bracelets, rings, necklaces, earrings, nose-rings, and tiaras. Sometimes it was all worn at the same time! Jewellery was made from gold, silver, bronze, ivory, precious jewels and glass.

PERFUME

Perfume was made by crushing flower petals, such as jasmine or rose, and mixing them with oil. Herbs and spices were used in the same way.

At parties, women might be given cones of perfume. They put them on their heads, where the scented oil dripped a fragrant perfume on their clothes.

Scented oils and creams were rubbed on the body to protect against sunburn and insect bites.

HAIRSTYLES

In Old Testament times, men and women wore their hair long. By the time of Jesus, many Jewish men had short hair and beards. But they didn't cut their sideburns, so these grew into long tassel-like lengths of hair.

Women did not usually wear their hair loose in public. They used curlers, hair-pins, hair-nets, and gold, ivory and wooden combs. They twisted their hair into tight curls. They also plaited their hair and put flowers, ribbons and jewels in it.

Bartering for goods

Bible Search

- A very rich man:
  Job 1:2–3
- Buying a slave:
  Hosea 3:2
- Lambs for money:
  2 Kings 3:4
- Abraham buys a field:
  Genesis 23:16

COUNTING SHEEP

A conquered nation paid taxes with farm produce as well as with silver and gold. King Mesha of Moab gave the king of Israel 100,000 lambs and the wool of 100,000 rams.

MONEY
IN OLD TESTAMENT TIMES

F or much of the Old Testament period, there was no money as we know it. At first, people got the things they wanted by bartering, that is, by swapping or trading. But this had snags. It was hard to work out what was fair. How much corn did you trade for five sheep?

THE FIRST COINS

In about 600 BC, Croesus, the King of Lydia (present-day western Turkey) hit on the idea of making gold coins and stamping them with their weight. The idea quickly caught on.

Coins were used to pass on news. When a new king came to power, he minted coins with the image of his head on them, to tell the world who he was. Poor countries made coins of copper or bronze.

THE FIRST MONEY

As well as bartering, people began to pay with silver jewellery or pieces of gold and silver. Hosea bought his wife back from slavery with silver and barley.

SHEKELS OF SILVER

Gold was not as common as silver, so it was more precious. Gold was used for payment between kings.

The Old Testament word for money is 'silver'. Silver and gold were weighed on scales and measured in shekels and talents. 'Shekel' comes from a word meaning 'weigh'. 'Talent' meant a large amount.

Gold and silver

MONEY
IN NEW TESTAMENT TIMES

B y the time the New Testament was written, there were Roman, Greek and Jewish coins circulating in Palestine. All had different values, so shopping could be rather confusing. There was plenty of work for the money-changers.

ROMAN MONEY

Roman taxes had to be paid with Roman money:

- Quadran. The smallest Roman coin, made of bronze.
- As. One as was worth four quadrans. It was made of bronze. In Matthew we read that two sparrows cost one as.

- Denarius. This was a large silver coin, worth sixteen times more than one as. Matthew tells us that a workman was paid one denarius for a day's work.

Denarius

- Sparrows: *Matthew 10:29*
- Workman's wage: *Matthew 20:1–16*
- The king's servants: *Luke 19:12–27*
- A poor widow: *Luke 21:1–4*

GREEK COINS

- Drachma. One drachma was worth one Roman denarius. It was made of silver.
- Didrachma. A silver coin worth two drachmas. Taxes due to the Temple were paid in didrachmas because they contained more silver than Roman coins.
- Tetradrachma or stater. One tetradrachma was worth four drachmas. This coin was made of silver. The thirty pieces of silver paid to Judas were probably tetradrachmas.

Tetradrachma

- Mina. A silver coin worth 100 drachmas. In Luke there is a story about a king giving his servants ten minas (about three months' wages).

JEWISH MONEY

- Lepton. This was the smallest possible coin, worth half a Roman quadran. In Luke we read about a widow who gave all she had to the collection in the Temple: two lepta.

The widow in Luke's story

- A talent. This was not a coin. It meant a large amount of money.

LOOKING AFTER MONEY

There were no safes, and probably no banks. To keep their money safe, people buried it in the ground or put it in the Temple treasury in Jerusalem.

Archaeologists have found hoards of money, often in clay pots, buried in the ground.

Money was buried in the ground

MUSIC AND INSTRUMENTS

The Israelites filled their lives with music. They became so good at music-making that their fame spread to other countries. When King Sennacherib of Assyria attacked Jerusalem, he took away with him silver, gold, and male and female singers. We know this because he boasted about it in his court records!

PLENTY OF RHYTHM

Usually, songwriters took well-known tunes and put new words to them. Musicians improvised on the tunes as they played.

Tunes were not very tuneful. Mostly, the songs and hymns were chanted. Often the singers sang alternate lines. But what the songs lacked in tune, they made up for in rhythm. The music was great for dancing to!

INSTRUMENTS

There were all sorts of instruments: timbrels, trumpets, horns, pipes, sistrums, lyres, cymbals, lutes and flutes.

TIMBREL
A timbrel, or tambourine, was made from animal skin stretched over a hoop.

TRUMPET
There were different kinds of trumpet. The shofar was a long horn which turned up at the end. It was used to call people to battle or to worship.

HORN
The horn, or cornet, was one of the instruments that Joshua's priests blew when they attacked Jericho.

PIPE
A pipe probably made a wailing, moaning sound. It was played at funerals.

LYRE
A lyre, or harp, was the instrument David played.

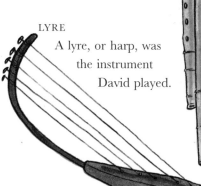

LARGE LYRE
The sound box of this instrument was probably round and flat, and it would have made a low, rich sound.

SISTRUM
This was rather like a baby's rattle.

CYMBALS
'Loud cymbals' were two shallow metal plates which were clashed together. 'High sounding cymbals' were hollow metal cups.

LUTE
A lute was shaped like a triangle, with three strings.

FLUTE
The Hebrew word for 'flute' means 'hiss' or 'whistle'.

Bible Search

- A victory song: *Exodus 15*
- A king's wedding song: *Psalm 45*
- A sad song: *2 Samuel 1:17–27*
- A marching song: *Numbers 10:35*

OLIVES AND VINES

Olive trees were called 'the king of trees'. Fresh or pickled olives were eaten with bread, but most olives were made into oil.

Bible teachers often called the Israelites 'God's vine'. God planted them, looked after them, and wanted them to produce 'good grapes'.

GROWING OLIVES

Olive trees lived for many hundreds of years, but for the first fifteen years, a tree had no fruit.

To harvest the olives, the branches of the tree were beaten with poles. The olives were gathered into baskets and taken to stone olive presses. A large round stone, turned by a man or donkey, squeezed out the oil. The olive pulp was then put into baskets and pressed with weights. Heavier weights were added to get out as much oil as possible.

USES OF OLIVE OIL

Olive oil was used:

● For cooking.

● To burn in lamps.
● As a hair and skin tonic.

● As a medicine to put on wounds.

● As a scent (it was perfumed first!)

● For anointing. Olive oil was poured over someone's head as a sign that the person was specially chosen to do work for God. Objects could be anointed too.

GROWING VINES

The young vine plants were set out in rows, often in terraces on the hillside. A watchtower was built in the vineyard, so a lookout could be kept for wild animals and thieves.

The vine harvest was a happy time. Families camped out in the vineyards. Ripe bunches of grapes were cut with small hooks and put into baskets.

Grapes were made into wine in wine presses, which were often stone hollows in the vineyards. The workers sang songs as they trampled the grapes with their bare feet. The juice was collected in goatskins or jars, and left to ferment into wine.

As well as being used to make wine, grapes were dried, and pressed together to make raisin cakes.

Bible Search

● The vine and God's people: *Isaiah 5:1–7*

● Jesus the true vine: *John 15:1–8*

● A good person is like an olive tree: *Psalm 52:8*

PAINTING
AND SCULPTURE

I n the Ten Commandments, God told the Israelites not to make or worship idols. They understood this to mean that they should not paint, draw, or make a model of any human being, animal, bird or fish. This didn't leave much to paint! Not surprisingly, the Israelites had little interest in painting and sculpture. They were creative in other ways, such as in literature and music, and possibly in embroidery, jewellery and carving.

TOMBS

Egyptian artists painted colourful scenes of everyday life on the walls of their tombs. They thought that these scenes would magically come to life in the spirit world.

But the Jews did not think like this. Hundreds of tombs have been excavated, but only one contains a painting, and that was made much later than the time of the New Testament.

An Egyptian tomb painting

DECORATION

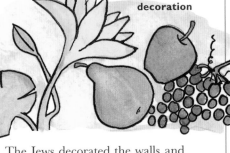

A wall decoration

The Jews decorated the walls and pillars of their synagogues with drawings of plants, flowers, palm trees and fruit, or with objects from the Temple, such as the seven-branched candlestick, and scrolls.

Greek vases were decorated with beautiful pictures. But pots made in Palestine were painted, not very skilfully, with zigzag lines and simple patterns.

A Greek pot

THE TABERNACLE

When they were slaves in Egypt, the Israelites learnt many artistic skills from the Egyptians. They used these skills to make the Tabernacle, the worship tent. They believed that their artistic abilities were given by God. But they didn't pass on their skills to their children. When Solomon built the Temple in Jerusalem, he employed craftsmen from Phoenicia.

CHERUBIM

The Ark of the Covenant (the box containing the Ten Commandments) had two cherubim on the top.

There were two gold cherubim in the Most Holy Place of the Temple built by Solomon. They were winged creatures, possibly with a human body and a lion's head.

Bible Search

- A nightmare wall painting: *Ezekiel 8:10*
- Making an idol: *Isaiah 40:19–20; 44:12–14*
- A gift from God: *Exodus 35:30–35*
- Cherubim in the Temple: *1 Kings 6:23–28*

A pot from Palestine

PHARISEES
A VERY RELIGIOUS PEOPLE

The Pharisees were a group of very religious people, who kept the Jewish laws very strictly. In New Testament times, there were 6,000 Pharisees. They were powerful people, because everybody looked up to them. Many were members of the Sanhedrin, a council of religious leaders in Jerusalem. The Sanhedrin had the power to judge, punish and imprison people brought before it.

A Pharisee

Bible Search

- A good Pharisee: *John 3:1–2*
- A story: *Luke 18:9–14*
- Whitewashed tombs: *Matthew 23:1–27*
- Washing: *Mark 7:1–8*

LAWS

The first five books of the Bible, which the Jews called the Torah, or Law, contain 613 different laws. Bible teachers divided the Law up into many thousands of little rules. They called these rules 'the teaching of the elders'. Pharisees kept every rule.

WASHING

Pharisees said that before every meal your hands had to be washed. This was a sign that you wanted to be clean from wrong. They laid down strict rules about how to wash your hands. The rules were too strict for most people. Jesus said, 'What's the use of having clean hands if your hearts are full of anger and greed?'

The Pharisees' rules were like burdens, and their law was often called a yoke. (A yoke was a frame put on two oxen pulling a plough.) Jesus said, 'Come to me all you who are burdened. …My yoke is easy.'

Washing

JESUS AND PHARISEES

Some Pharisees were good men. But some thought they were better than everyone else.

Some Pharisees thought they were better than every-body else

Jesus and the Pharisees had many head-on clashes. Jesus once described them as 'whitewashed tombs'. He meant they looked nice on the outside, but inside they were rotten.

A white-washed tomb

Jesus told a story about a Pharisee and a tax-collector. The Pharisee thanked God for making him good. The tax-collector asked for forgiveness. Jesus said that God accepted the tax-collector, but not the Pharisee.

SHOW-OFFS

The Pharisees were not very popular. People thought they showed off by having extra-long tassels on their prayer shawls. People grumbled that the Pharisees chose the best seats for themselves in meetings.

Telling stories over a meal

PLAYS,
BOOKS AND ENTERTAINMENTS

In Bible times, people did not go out in the evening for entertainment, as people may do today. They relaxed over meals, making music or telling stories.

Religious festivals drew big crowds at holiday times, and by New Testament times, the Greeks and Romans had introduced big sports contests or gladiator fights.

THEATRE

The Greeks loved the theatre. Some Greek writers wrote clever comedies; others wrote serious plays to make people feel very sad, angry or scared.

Greek theatres were all open-air. The audience sat on rows of stone seats, built in a semi-circle, which faced a stage made out of stone.

A Greek theatre

PLAYS

Most Jews refused to go to Greek plays. We know of one Jewish writer of plays. His name was Ezekiel, and he lived in Alexandria in Egypt, before Jesus was born. He wrote plays based on Bible stories.

- A dancing display: *Mark 6:22*
- A public meeting: *Acts 19:29*
- Party music: *Amos 6:5*
- Prizes for riddles: *Judges 14:12–13*
- Music and dancing: *Luke 15:25*

ONE-MAN THEATRE

Jewish teachers, or rabbis, gave talks in public places. If a teacher didn't have a voice which carried well, he had a herald who repeated what he said, rather like a human loudspeaker.

These talks were not boring lectures. The speakers used poetry, short stories, proverbs, humour, rhymes and catchy sayings to get over their main points. The teacher Gamaliel once used 300 examples to illustrate one point.

The best example of this sort of speaking is Jesus' talks to the people.

LIBRARIES

In Palestine in Jesus' time, there were private libraries of Old Testament scrolls and other religious writings, but no public libraries.

PARTIES

The Jews often had parties. When all the food was cleared away, there was music and dancing. Men and women danced separately. People told stories, jokes and riddles, and talked for hours.

At big Roman parties, there would be entertainment between the courses of the meal. This might be prose and poetry readings, music, and dancing displays.

Men and women danced separately

POTTERS
IMPORTANT CRAFTSMEN

E very village had a potter. He was important because of the useful things he made: jugs, bowls, pots, storage jars, lamps and seals for letters.

Clay was dug from the ground and stamped on to get all the air out of it. It was then mixed with water and some grit.

SHAPING CLAY

Working with clay

Clay was shaped by hand. The first clay bowls were made by putting long coils known as 'worms' of clay on top of each other to build up a shape. The sides were then smoothed down. The pot was left to dry, then decorated and baked in a kiln.

Some potters used a potter's wheel. The wheel was a stone which was placed in another hollowed-out stone. One man turned the top stone while the potter worked the clay.

A potter's wheel that could be turned by foot was not invented until about 200 years before Jesus' time.

Potters sometimes pressed clay into wooden moulds. Seals and oil lamps were made in this way.

Bible Search

- Trampling clay: **Isaiah 41:25**
- Jeremiah: **Jeremiah 18:1–6**
- A seal on clay: **Job 38:14**

Using a potter's wheel

DECORATION

These were some methods of decorating a pot:
- A woven rope was pressed into the wet clay.
- When the clay was dry, but not hard, the pot could be chiselled or engraved.
- Coloured clay might be added in bands or zigzag patterns as the pot was being made. Red and black were popular colours.
- A pot could be burnished to make it shine. Before it was fired, the dry pot was put on the wheel, and turned whilst holding a piece of pottery or bone against it.

FIRING

Once a pot had been dried and decorated, it was baked, or fired. A simple kiln might be shelves over a fire. Some kilns were dome-shaped clay ovens in a 1.25 m (4 ft) deep, 3 m (10 ft) wide hole in the ground.

PRIDE
AND HUMILITY

A proud person might think, 'I am in control of my own life. I don't need or want God.' A humble person says, 'I am weak, and do wrong things. I need God's help.' The Book of Proverbs has wise words about pride: 'Pride leads to arguments, but those who take advice are wise. Pride goes before destruction, and a haughty spirit before a fall.'

Pride goes before a fall

MARY'S SONG

When Mary knew that she was going to be the mother of Jesus, she sang a song in praise of God: 'God has scattered those who are proud in their innermost thoughts… but has lifted up the humble.'

Mary praises God

JESUS

Jesus described himself as gentle and humble in heart. This didn't mean he was weak, but that he had great strength, controlled by God. When Jesus was on trial before his enemies, they made fun of him, but he didn't let them make him angry.

RUDE GUESTS

People who think they are good are in for a nasty shock. This was the point of Jesus' story about rude guests. A rich man invited important guests to his feast, and they all made excuses. So he invited blind people, cripples and beggars: people who were usually despised.

Jesus was making the point that proud people may refuse God's call to join him. But people who don't think they deserve God's love will be thrilled to find that he cares for them.

PAUL

Paul had a problem with pride. He had a lot to be proud about. He boasted that he had been a perfect Jew. He boasted about how much he had suffered for Jesus. God had to keep on pulling him down to size!

Paul wrote about how stupid he felt in the town of Damascus. There were guards at the city gates waiting to arrest him. The only way Paul could escape was by being let down over the city walls in a basket.

Paul wrote: 'God chose the weak things of the world… so that no one may boast.'

Bible Search

- Paul boasts:
  2 Corinthians 11:16–33;
  Philippians 3:3–10

- Jesus: *1 Peter 2:23;*
  Matthew 11:29

- Rude guests: *Luke 14:16–21*

- God chooses weak people:
  1 Corinthians 1:26–28

The rich man welcomes his guests

SABBATH A DAY OF REST

T he word 'Sabbath' comes from the Hebrew word for seven. The fourth of the Ten Commandments says, 'Remember the Sabbath day by keeping it holy… On it you shall not do any work.' The Jews took this command seriously. Every seventh day was a day for praise and worship.

THE SABBATH

The Sabbath began when it got dark on Friday evening, and ended at the same time on Saturday evening. (A new day started in the evening, not at midnight.) To let everyone know when the Sabbath had begun and ended, a trumpeter would go to the top of the tallest building and blow some loud notes.

A trumpeter

GETTING READY

Each Friday, houses were cleaned and food was cooked, because no cooking was to be done on the Sabbath. Then everyone washed and put on their best clothes. Lamps were lit and the whole family sat down for a meal.

Food was cooked on Friday

- The fourth commandment: *Exodus 20:8–11*

- Jesus and the Sabbath: *Mark 2:23–3:6*

- Trumpets for alarm clocks: *Leviticus 25:9*

SATURDAY

In Jesus' time, on Saturday morning everyone went to the synagogue for Bible reading, teaching and prayers.

There were thousands of rules to stop people doing things which might be considered as work.
- A writer could not carry his pen in case he 'worked' and wrote something.
- No one was allowed to eat an egg that a hen had laid on the Sabbath.
- If your donkey fell down a well, you could lift it out. But you could only help an injured person if his life was in danger.

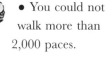

- You could not walk more than 2,000 paces.

ARGUMENTS

In the time of Jesus, teachers argued about these laws. Some said they were too strict; others said they were not strict enough. The Essene community (a group of very religious Jews) thought that it was better to let a man drown than to rescue him on the Sabbath.

One Sabbath, Jesus healed a man's hand. Jesus said, 'The Sabbath was made for man, not man for the Sabbath.'

Essenes believed that a drowning man couldn't be rescued on the Sabbath

52

SACRIFICES

AN OFFERING TO GOD

Sometimes the Jews forgot the need to feel sorry too

A sacrifice was something valuable which was given to God to say 'thank you' or 'sorry'. It was also a way of making a promise to God. It was an outward sign of an inner feeling. Sometimes the Jews forgot this, and thought the outward sign was enough, without the need to feel sorry or thankful. This was wrong.

ANIMAL SACRIFICE

The Old Testament taught that sin must be punished. People believed that by killing an animal, their own sins would be forgiven. Only sheep, goats, cattle or doves could be sacrificed. They had to be young and perfect. These animals were known as 'clean' animals.

The person making the sacrifice put his hands on the animal. Then he gave the animal to the priest. The priest killed it and sprinkled its blood on the altar. This showed the animal's life was given instead of the life of the sinful person. The worshipper was forgiven and could be at peace with God.

Offerings of grain were sometimes made as well. The first food harvested each year was also offered to God to give thanks.

TYPES OF SACRIFICE

● Burnt offering. A whole animal was burnt. This meant that you gave your life to God.

A burnt offering

● A grain offering was an accompaniment to fellowship and burnt offerings. Flour, bread, grain and incense were offered. The priest burnt some and kept the rest.
● A fellowship offering was a sign of friendship with God. The fatty parts of an animal were burnt. The priest kept some and the rest was roasted and eaten in a family meal.
● A sin offering allowed a sinner to be forgiven. An animal was killed and its blood was sprinkled on the altar.
● For a guilt offering, the fatty parts of the animal were burnt. The priests kept the rest. These offerings might be made by someone who had been stealing, or someone who had broken God's law by mistake, or by a leper who had been healed.

ALTARS

A sacrifice was made on an altar. At first, altars were a mound of earth, a block of stone, or a flat stone supported by other stones. In time, 'horns' shaped like animal's horns were added at the four corners of a stone block.

A grain offering

Bible Search

● God's laws: *Leviticus 17:11*

● Jesus' sacrifice: *Hebrews 9:26–28*

● What God really wants: *Hosea 6:6*

SCHOOLS
AND TEACHERS

For the Jews, school meant learning about God. Every lesson was religious education. When Jesus was alive, school was not compulsory. Girls were not allowed to go to school, and had to stay at home and learn how to run a house.

Girls had to learn how to run a home

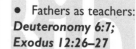

- Fathers as teachers:
Deuteronomy 6:7;
Exodus 12:26–27
- Jesus listens in on a lesson:
Luke 2:41–47
- Paul in higher education:
Acts 22:3

HIGHER EDUCATION

A father teaches his son

HOME EDUCATION

At home, mothers would tell their children stories from the Old Testament, and fathers might teach God's laws, the commandments, and the meaning of the religious festivals.

Learning at home

SYNAGOGUE SCHOOLS

At the age of five or six, boys went to school in the local synagogue. These synagogue schools were called 'houses of the book', because all the lessons were from the Old Testament.

Each synagogue had one classroom. This was the room where the Old Testament scrolls were kept. The teacher sat on a small platform, and the children sat on the floor in front of him.

If there were more than forty children in the class, the teacher had to have a helper.

Children learned long passages of the Old Testament off by heart. They may also have learned to read and write from the Bible.

Teachers were paid by the synagogue. They were considered to be very important people, and were called 'messengers of the Almighty'. But if they were too strict, they were sacked!

At thirteen, boys left school. Most started working with their father, joining him in whatever trade he followed. A father would teach his son the skills he needed for the job, which probably also included arithmetic. If a boy wanted to learn how to be a teacher, he had to go to Jerusalem, where teachers (mostly Pharisees) held lectures in the Temple courts. Learning was by discussion and argument.

Discussion and argument

SCIENCE
LOOKING AT THE WORLD

Science is the study of the world around us, and the laws which control it. People study science for the excitement of knowing how things work, and use their knowledge to find ways to make life better on Earth.

We still use the Greeks' discoveries today

MESOPOTAMIA

In ancient Mesopotamia (the land Abraham came from), people loved to study maths and astronomy. Their number system was based on the number sixty. Our time measurements of sixty minutes to an hour, and sixty seconds to a minute, come from the Mesopotamian system.

The earliest picture we have of a wheel comes from southern Mesopotamia. It's a pictogram dating from 3500 BC, and shows a sledge with wheels.

Studying the stars

EGYPT AND ISRAEL

The pyramids

The Egyptians were interested in sciences which aimed to ensure a good life in the next world, such as embalming and the building of pyramids.

The Jews were not very interested in science. They believed that only God knew the secret of why things were as they were. They believed it was more important to study the Bible than to study the world.

When Bible writers wrote about natural events in the world, they described them in poetry, not scientific language. The events were recorded in order to praise God.

GREEKS AND ROMANS

The Greeks were great scientists and mathematicians. In about 550 BC, Pythagoras worked out how scientific investigations should be made: by looking carefully, doing experiments, and forming conclusions based on the results.

The Romans took up Greek ideas and discoveries, and became great engineers.

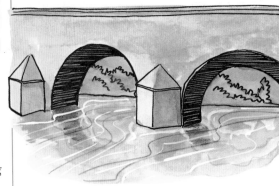

A Roman aqueduct

Bible Search

- God knows the law of the world: *Job 38*

- Astronomers: *Matthew 2:1–12*

- A poem: *Psalm 19:1–6*

SCRIBES
TEACHERS OF THE LAW

A scribe

S cribes were the readers, writers and accountants of ancient times, so they were important people. In the New Testament, the scribes are called 'teachers of the Law', Rabbi, and 'experts in the Law'. (The Law was their Bible, and is now our Old Testament.)

WRITERS

Getting a letter written by a scribe

At first, only priests and scribes could read and write. People went to a scribe to get a letter written or read. A scribe always carried his writing equipment with him: reed pens in a pen case, and an ink horn hanging from his belt. He also had a knife for cutting paper.

A scribe reads out a letter

KINGS' MEN AND LAWYERS

Kings depended on scribes to write up court records, to keep account of taxes, and make lists. Scribes also acted as their advisers.

Scribes would sit by the city gates, a spot where business was conducted. They acted as lawyers, and could write out a will or legal document there and then.

THE EXILE

When the people of Judah were taken as prisoners to Babylonia, although they no longer had their Temple, scribes copied out the Law and taught it to the people. The most famous scribe, who was also a priest, was Ezra. Without the scribes, the people of Judah might have lost their sense of being God's special people.

Bible Search

- Jesus: *Matthew 23*
- Shebna the scribe: *2 Kings 18:18*
- Gamaliel: *Acts 5:33–39*.

NEW TESTAMENT

In the New Testament, scribes are called 'teachers of the Law'. They worked out many rules, which they said people had to keep. These were passed on by word of mouth (called the 'oral law').

They also trained young people to become teachers of the Law. Anybody, rich or poor, could join their classes, which were held in the Temple.

Some scribes were members of the Sanhedrin, a council of religious leaders in Jerusalem.

JESUS

Many teachers of the Law didn't like Jesus because he wouldn't keep all the extra rules. Jesus said, 'You shut the kingdom of heaven in men's faces.'

SERVANTS
AND SLAVES

S ervants were really slaves. A slave was his owner's property. Some owners looked after their slaves, but many did not.

Foreign slaves were bought in the slave market or captured in war. Thieves who could not pay back the money they had stolen, were forced to be slaves. Sometimes poor

A cruel master

people sold themselves or their children into slavery to pay off debts. It was forbidden to force a fellow Israelite to be a slave against his will.

Selling children to be slaves

Slaves had certain rights. These included:

A lost tooth

● A slave must not be killed.
● If an owner hit his slave so hard that the slave lost an eye, or a tooth, the slave had to be set free.

The Sabbath was a rest day

● Slaves had to have the Sabbath as a rest day.

● An Israelite slave could buy himself free at any time.
● After six years, an Israelite slave was always set free, and had to be given money and help.
● A slave was not allowed to work more than ten hours a day.
● If a slave ran away, and hid with someone, that person could not hand him over to his master.

A runaway slave

IN NEW TESTAMENT TIMES

Laws to protect Jewish slaves were so strict that there was a saying, 'Whoever buys a Jewish slave gives himself a master.' Probably, most Jewish slaves in Palestine were former thieves. Rich Jews had foreign slaves.

'Whoever buys a Jewish slave gives himself a master.'

ROMAN AND GREEK SLAVES

The Roman and Greek way of life depended on slaves. It has been said there were 60,000,000 (60 million) slaves in the Roman empire. Often, slaves were not considered to be people. A Roman called Varro said a slave was 'a kind of tool that can speak'. An owner could do whatever he liked with his slaves.

Bible Search

● Slave laws:
Deuteronomy 23:15–16;
Exodus 21:26–27

● Testing a slave:
Luke 12:42–46

● A wage dispute:
Matthew 20:1–16

SHEPHERDS
AND NOMADS

A trumpet made from a horn

When God called Abraham to leave Ur and go to live in Canaan, Abraham became a nomad. He began to live a wandering life, moving from one water spring to another with his flocks, and living in a tent.

When the Israelites settled in Canaan, their flocks were very important. The sheep and goats provided milk, food, and wool for clothes. Skins were made into leather, and horns were used as trumpets and containers for oil.

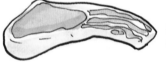

Goat's meat

Goat's milk

SHEPHERDS AT WORK

A shepherd's life was hard. There was danger from wild animals, robbers and enemy soldiers. If a sheep was hurt or tired, the shepherd carried it on his shoulders.

Today, shepherds often drive sheep along with the help of dogs. In Bible times, a shepherd led the way, and his sheep followed him. He often gave each sheep its own name, and the sheep came when he called.

A robber

TOOLS FOR THE JOB

A shepherd had certain equipment to help in his work:
- A strong club with flints (later nails) in the thick end, to attack marauders.
- A sling. This was used to fire stones at wild animals which threatened attack.
- A small leather bag to hold stones for the sling.
- A staff. This was a long stick with a curve at one end, to control the sheep.
- A pipe. Often a shepherd would call his sheep by playing a few notes on his pipe.

A shepherd

SHEEPFOLD

A shepherd sleeps outside his sheepfold

During the winter months, sheep were brought down to the village, and kept in a strong-walled sheepfold.

In summer, the sheep stayed out on the hills. At night they had to be kept safe. If the shepherd couldn't find a cave, he built a sheepfold from stones, with brambles on the top to make a roof. Instead of a door, the shepherd lay across the entrance.

PSALM 23

Psalm 23 is a poem about a shepherd's care for his sheep. In this psalm, God is compared to a loving shepherd. Jesus later called himself the Good Shepherd.

- Nomads:
Deuteronomy 26:5
- Calling a sheep:
John 10:3–5
- The door:
John 10:7
- The good shepherd:
John 10:11–21

Bible Search

SHOPS
AND TRADERS

Trading with other countries

King Solomon became rich from trading with other countries. His example encouraged people in Jerusalem and Samaria to start trading. The prophet Amos, writing about 760 BC, said the tradesmen were so greedy for money that they hated holidays, because work had to stop.

BIG BUSINESS

About 600 BC, Babylon was the trading centre of the world. During the time the Jews were exiled in Babylonia, they learnt business and banking skills. Archaeologists have found the records of some very rich Jewish traders.

MARKETS

In Bible times, there were no shops in small towns. People went to the city markets to buy olive oil, fish, figs, grapes, wine, animals, clothes, material and pottery. Market inspectors had the job of checking the traders' scales, and making sure that prices were fair.

Bible Search

- Greedy traders: *Amos 8:5*
- Putting money in a bank: *Matthew 25:27*
- Advice to businessmen: *James 4:13–15*
- Shopping in Rome: *Revelation 18:11–13*
- Personal loans: *Luke 6:34–35*

Shops in Jerusalem

MONEY-CHANGERS

People from all over the world came to Palestine, and money-changers were kept busy. They charged a fee which equalled about ten per cent of the value of the money they changed.

All Jews had to pay a tax to the Temple in Jerusalem. Unfortunately, the money-changers in the Temple often cheated their customers. Jesus described the Temple as a robbers' den. Money-changers also lent money. The table on which they put their money was called a 'bank'. They lent money to people such as those setting up new businesses, shipbuilders, and international traders.

Checking a trader's scales

SHOPS

By the time of Jesus, there were probably small shops in Jerusalem and the larger cities, crowded side by side along the narrow streets.

Shops selling the same products would have been grouped together.

A bank

SOLDIERS
IN THE OLD TESTAMENT

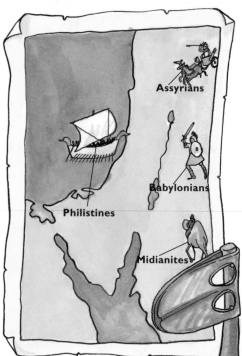

The Israelites took the Promised Land of Canaan by force: they were the invading army. After that time, they themselves were often invaded by other armies, and beaten.

God sometimes chose unusual battle tactics to teach the Israelites to rely on him.

WEAPONS

- For hand-to-hand fighting: axes, clubs, swords.
- For long-distance attack: slings, javelins, bows and arrows. The arrows were made out of reed, with metal heads. A quiver carried thirty arrows.

An archer

- For defence: chain mail (metal 'scales' sewn to cloth), and shields (a wooden frame covered with leather).

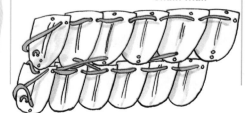

Chain mail

ENEMIES OF THE ISRAELITES

- Philistines. The Philistine warriors were the dreaded enemy at the time the Book of Judges was written. They took away all blacksmiths from the land, so that the people could not make iron weapons.
- Assyrians. The Assyrians often went on raids to get money to build magnificent temples and palaces.
- Babylonians. If an enemy would not give in quietly, the Babylonian army took them all off as prisoners of war, leaving behind only the very poorest people.
- Midianites. The Midianites and other desert fighters swooped in on camels.

The Midianites

BATTLE TACTICS

- An ambush. The Israelites were particularly good at surprising and tricking their enemies. King David conquered Jerusalem by sending a few soldiers up an underground tunnel.
- Laying siege to a town. Towns were protected by thick walls (sometimes by two walls), with towers and ditches round the outside. A town would be surrounded and the army either waited until the people ran out of food and gave in, or broke down the walls.
- One-to-one combat. Often, a battle between two armies was decided by a duel between one champion from each army, such as between David and the Philistine giant Goliath.

Bible Search

- Chain mail: *1 Kings 22:34*
- Spies: *Joshua 2:1–7*
- King Uzziah's weapons: *2 Chronicles 26:14*
- Invaders besiege Jerusalem: *Isaiah 36:1–3*

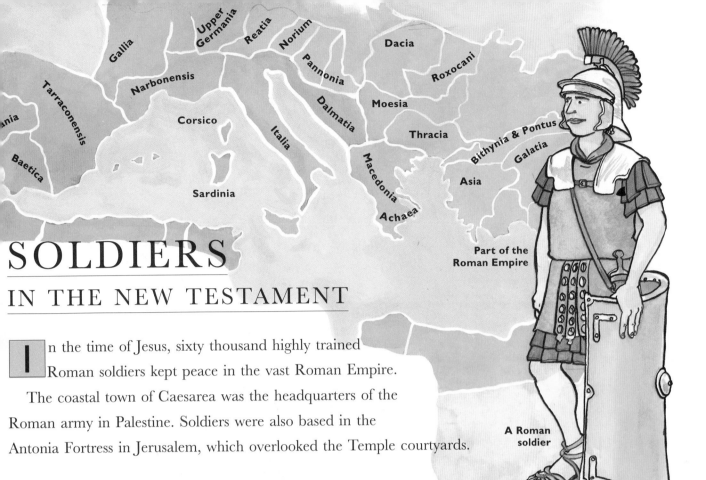

Part of the
Roman Empire

A Roman
soldier

SOLDIERS
IN THE NEW TESTAMENT

In the time of Jesus, sixty thousand highly trained Roman soldiers kept peace in the vast Roman Empire. The coastal town of Caesarea was the headquarters of the Roman army in Palestine. Soldiers were also based in the Antonia Fortress in Jerusalem, which overlooked the Temple courtyards.

ROMAN SOLDIERS

Sword and dagger

A Roman soldier would have:
- A double-edged sword, used in hand-to-hand fighting.
- A dagger.
- A shield made from wood, covered with leather and edged with metal.
- A bronze and iron helmet covering the neck and ears.
- Armour made from scales wired to each other and sewn on to cloth or leather.
- A spear.

Centurions were Roman officers in charge of a hundred soldiers. They were well-paid, intelligent men. Centurions made the Roman army into the successful force that it was.

JEWS AND WAR

Jews were not allowed to join the Roman army.

Jewish freedom fighters hid in the northern hills. The fiercest, the Sicarii, were a sort of assassination squad. Their name came from the short curved dagger which they hid under their cloaks. During festivals, they mixed with the crowds and stabbed Roman sympathizers.

The Jews were waiting for a Messiah (a king) who would rescue them from the Romans. Sometimes, somebody would come along claiming to be this great leader. He would collect a gang of followers and start fighting the Romans. But the Romans would send in their cavalry and squash the rebellion.

THE JEWISH WAR

In AD 66, about thirty years after Jesus died, the whole country rose up against Roman power. There was horrific fighting and bloodshed. The Roman army finally destroyed Jerusalem in AD 70. Jesus had warned his friends that this would happen, and had told them to escape to the hills.

- A centurion:
Luke 7:2–10

- Paul is rescued:
Acts 21:27–36

- False Messiahs:
Acts 5:35–39; Mark 13:21–22

- A warning of war:
Mark 13:14–19

Bible Search

SPORTS AND GAMES

Wrestling

In Old Testament times, archery and wrestling contests were popular. The Israelites were experts at using the sling as a weapon of war, and boys liked to play 'slings and stones'.

In New Testament times, the Greeks and Romans loved sports, and so did many of the Jews. Pharisees didn't approve of the Greek games, because they were religious events, held in praise of the god Zeus. Roman sports were bloodthirsty, and the Jews despised them.

GREEK GAMES

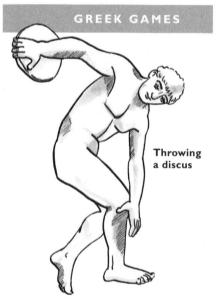

Throwing a discus

The Greeks thought physical fitness was as important as education. They held all sorts of contests. The pentathlon events were long jump, running, discus, javelin and wrestling. Greek boxing was a fight to the death. Instead of boxing gloves, arms and hands were bound with leather studded with metal.

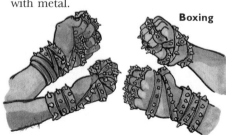

Boxing

OLYMPIC GAMES

Greeks held the first Olympic Games in the village of Olympia in 776 BC, for the god Zeus. The games were held every four years, and while they took place, all warfare stopped. Only men were allowed to watch the Olympic Games: any woman who watched was put to death. After 392 BC, the Games stopped. They were started again only a hundred years ago, in 1894.

* Sling shots:
Judges 20:16
* Wrestling:
Genesis 32:22–32
* Strict training:
I Corinthians 9:24–27
* A race:
Hebrews 12:1–2

Bible Search

ROMAN SPORTS

Chariot racing

In chariot races, a team of four trained horses pulled two-wheeled chariots for seven laps round a stadium. The drivers tied the horses' reins around their bodies.

Some Roman sports were very bloodthirsty. Gladiators fought with swords, or nets, or on horseback. Sometimes they fought in teams. The fight would not end until all the members of one team were dead. Criminals or slaves were often made to be gladiators.

Another cruel spectator sport was forcing people to fight wild animals. They were put into an arena, and a pack of starving animals was set loose on them. This was often the fate of criminals, but it also happened to Christians in Rome.

A wild animal

A synagogue was often built on high ground

SYNAGOGUE

THE CENTRE OF JEWISH LIFE

The word synagogue means a meeting place for Jews. The synagogue was the town hall, day school, law court, community centre and welfare office. But chiefly it was the place where people went to learn about God and to pray.

IMPORTANT PLACES

When Jesus was alive, every village had a synagogue. Jerusalem had 394. The Jewish law said that a synagogue could be built wherever there were ten married Jewish men. So there were synagogues throughout the Roman world. Paul went to the synagogues on his travels, to tell people about Jesus.

Bible Search

- Guest preacher Jesus:
Luke 4:16–21
- Guest preacher Paul:
Acts 13:14–45
- Law courts:
Luke 12:11
- Community centres:
Acts 9:2

INSIDE THE SYNAGOGUE

Jewish teachers said that no one should live higher than a synagogue, so synagogues were built on high ground or part of the building was tall, such as a dome.

The synagogue leaders stood or sat on a raised platform with a reading desk facing Jerusalem. There was a large cupboard, with a curtain in front, called the Ark. Inside were the books of the Old Testament, written out on long scrolls. The Ark was placed to face towards Jerusalem. There were three doors, all facing Jerusalem. Only the men went in by the main door.

Inside a synagogue

GOING TO A SERVICE

Before the service, the floor was rubbed with water mixed with mint.

Men, and boys over thirteen, sat on benches or mats facing the platform. Women, girls and younger boys sat in a gallery, or on one side, behind a screen.

LARGER SYNAGOGUES

The seven-branched candlestick

In larger synagogues, there was a covered passageway with small rooms leading off it. These were used for classrooms or private rooms for guests.

The gallery where women and children sat was supported by columns. These were often decorated with simple paintings or carvings, perhaps of palms, vine leaves, or the seven-branched candlestick. Jews were not allowed to draw or carve people or animals.

63

TAX-COLLECTORS
AND TAXES

A tax is money paid to the government towards the cost of ruling a country. In New Testament times, tax-collectors collected taxes for the Romans. There were three sorts of tax: two (called direct and indirect) which were paid to the government; the third was a religious tax which was paid to the Temple at Jerusalem.

Paying tax

DIRECT AND INDIRECT TAXES

In Galilee, King Herod charged taxes on all sorts of things: on fishing, salt, olive oil, and on clothes.

In Judea, there was a tax on every male over thirteen. One day, Jesus' enemies asked him if they should pay the tax. They thought that if he answered 'Yes', the Jews would hate him. If he said 'No', the Romans would arrest him. Jesus said, 'Show me a coin.' It had Caesar's head on it. 'Give to Caesar what belongs to Caesar,' he said. 'And to God what belongs to God.'

Indirect taxes were taxes on goods people wanted to sell. Tax kiosks were set up on bridges, at town gates, at markets and crossroads.

Market taxes

Bible Search

- A tax riot: **Acts 5:37**

- Matthew the tax-collector: **Matthew 9:9**

- A tricky question: **Matthew 22:15–21**

- John the Baptist's advice to tax-collectors: **Luke 3:13**

TAX-COLLECTORS

The Romans divided the country into areas. In each area, businessmen made bids for the right to collect the taxes. The highest bidder agreed to pay the Romans a sum of money every year. Any money he took on top of that was his own. There was massive overcharging. Tax-collectors were loathed because they worked for the enemy, and were often thieves as well.

Tax-collectors

YOUR CART TOO

If you went to the market to sell figs, you were charged tax. If you didn't have many figs to sell, the tax-collector might decide to charge you for your cart, and for each wheel on your cart! He made up taxes to suit himself, and no one could prove that they weren't real taxes.

TEMPLE
IN THE NEW TESTAMENT

- Watch your step:
Ecclesiastes 5:1

- Jesus' friends admire the Temple: *Mark 13:1–2*

- The curtain split in two:
Matthew 27:51

I n 19 BC King Herod began to rebuild the Temple in Jerusalem. He didn't do it in order to worship God, but to make the people think he was a great man. His Temple was magnificent. In AD 56 it was finished. In AD 70 the Romans destroyed it.

First Herod built an enormous stone platform across the flat top of Mount Moriah. It was the largest structure in the ancient world, bigger than fifty American football pitches of today.

THE FORTRESS OF ANTONIA.
A Roman army barracks.

THE TEMPLE.
The walls and roof were covered with gold. There were golden spikes all over the roof to stop the birds landing. Inside the Temple were:
• **The Holy Place.** Thirty-eight rooms, built on three floors, led off the sides. They were entered by doors on their outside walls.
• **The Holy of Holies (or Most Holy Place).** This was dark and silent, empty except for a large block of bare stone.

OUTER WALL.
5 m (15 ft) thick.

NICANOR GATE.
No woman could go beyond this gate.

WOMEN'S COURT.
This is where Jesus saw a poor widow putting all her money in an offering box.

GREAT BRONZE GATES.
These may have been the 'beautiful gate' where Peter healed the lame man.

FOUR COVERED COURTYARDS.
One was for storing wood, and one for oil, wine and salt. The third was for lepers who had been healed, and the last for Nazirites, or holy men.

LOW STONE WALLS.
Notices on this wall said that any foreigner who went further would be killed.

COURT OF THE PRIESTS.
Only priests could go in here. This was where animals were sacrificed on an enormous stone block, so it was a noisy, smelly place.

MEN'S COURT.
This was for Jewish men only. It was long and narrow, separated from the next court by a low wall.

COURT OF THE GENTILES.
An immense court, where everyone could go. Round the sides there were covered walkways, with rows of marble columns supporting a cedarwood roof. The floors were made of coloured mosaic.

SOLOMON'S PORCH.
Here the Jews tried to stone Jesus when he said, 'The Father and I are one.'

PINNACLE (OR TOWER).
Probably the place where the Devil took Jesus in the second temptation.

ROYAL PORCH.
This is where tradesmen sold animals and birds for the sacrifices. Sometimes they spread out into the Court of the Gentiles, turning it into a marketplace.

BATH HOUSE.
For ceremonial washing.

STONE STEPS leading to the main entrances on the south side. These steps were wide and then narrow in turns, forcing the people to go up slowly.

TENTMAKERS
AND TANNERS

I n Greece and Rome, the rulers looked down on everyone who had to work for a living. It was the opposite in Palestine. 'He who does not teach his son a trade teaches him robbery,' they said. The apostle Paul wrote with pride that he earned money for himself and his friends by making tents.

HOW TO MAKE A TENT

This is how Abraham and his sons might have made a tent.
● Get some goat or camel skins.
● Sew them together. Attach wooden toggles around the edges.

● Drive poles into the ground.

● Place the skins over the poles.

A tent

● Tie a rope to the wooden toggles. Tie the other end of the rope to tent-pegs sunk into the ground.

GOATS' HAIR

In New Testament times, goats' hair was used to make tents. It was woven into very long strips. The hair of goats and camels was particularly good for making tents, as it was waterproof.

Paul came from Tarsus, close to Cilicia. Here the very best goats' hair, called cilicium, was found.

LEATHER-WORKERS

Even after tents were no longer made from animals' skins but from goats' hair, tentmakers were usually also craftsmen in leather. They made items such as water-bottles, belts, leather slings, helmets, shields and sandals.

TANNERS

Although Jews thought that it was good to work, some jobs were regarded more highly than others. Tanners were at the very bottom of the list. They had to work with dead bodies of animals, which the Jews thought were 'unclean' (made you unfit to worship God). Also, it was very smelly work! Tanners had to work outside towns and villages, in places where the wind would not blow smells back into the town.

A tanner would prepare a hide like this:
● Skin the animal.
● Remove hairs from the skin (by scraping, soaking and rubbing in lime).
● Soak the skin in water.
● Rub in animal manure.
● Hammer until soft and flat.

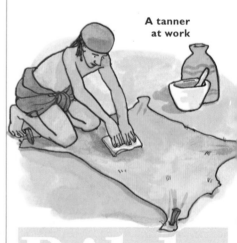

A tanner at work

Bible Search

● Paul: *Acts 18:3; 20:34*
● Peter: *Acts 9:43*
● Black goat's hair: *Song of Songs 1:5*
● Don't be idle: *2 Thessalonians 3:6–13*

TOWNS AND VILLAGES

Most people lived in villages. Villages were often very small, with perhaps only a few hundred people living there. In Old Testament times, the difference between a village and a town was that a town had a wall round it. By New Testament times, the difference was that a town had a court of law and judges. Towns and villages were usually built on hills.

VILLAGE LIFE

In Old Testament times, most village people were farmers. They worked in the fields surrounding the village, and sold their produce in the town markets. If an enemy attacked, the village people escaped to the nearest walled town.

TOWNS OR CITIES

Nearly all towns (sometimes called cities) in Old Testament times were small, with about 250 houses and 1,000 inhabitants. Houses were crowded together: sometimes you could cross a town by striding from one flat roof to another!

There were a few streets, and a maze of alleyways twisted between the houses. These often got filled with rubbish and sewage.

Crossing the town

MARKETS

Markets were held every day by the city gates. Craftsmen and traders sometimes put their goods on show outside their workshops. In larger towns, craftsmen were often grouped together on the same street.

CITY GATES

The noisy, crowded area round the city gates was the heart of the town. Each town had massive wooden gates, often covered with iron and bolted with strong bronze bars. Here business deals were made, lawsuits agreed, and notices nailed up. Beggars pleaded for help, and the city leaders met to talk.

ROMAN-STYLE TOWNS

A narrow street

Some of the towns we read about in the New Testament were built like Roman towns. King Herod rebuilt Samaria and Caesarea with a wide main street lined with shops and theatres, and smaller streets crossing neatly at right-angles. There were public baths, and the houses were built in blocks of four.

A market

Bible Search

- Walls: *Deuteronomy 1:28, 3:5*
- A fortified city: *Jeremiah 34:7*
- Street of the bakers: *Jeremiah 37:21*

TRAVEL
BY LAND

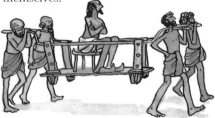

Travelling was uncomfortable and dangerous. It was easy to get lost, and there were many robbers who attacked travellers.

ROADS

In Old Testament times, the only roads were tracks. The tracks were given grand names, such as 'The Way of the Sea' and 'The King's Highway', but they didn't live up to their names. In 1200 BC, an Egyptian wrote that roads in Canaan were 'filled with boulders and pebbles...overgrown with reeds, thorns and brambles'.

When a king or ruler was travelling, someone would go ahead to repair the roads.

A road in Canaan

ROMAN ROADS

The Romans were the first to make good roads. Their 80,000 km (50,000 miles) of straight roads made as much impact on their world as the inventions of the train, car and plane have in this century. Roman armies and messengers could now travel quickly to any part of the empire.

Only soldiers and government messengers were allowed to use the roads. Other travellers had to walk alongside!

The roads were made of a layer of sand, a layer of stone, and a layer of crushed stones mixed with cement. This was topped with large paving stones sloping to gutters on each side. Mileposts were put up every 1,000 paces (1,480 m).

Roman shops sold maps showing the network of Roman roads.

A Roman road

TRANSPORT

Most people walked, or rode donkeys. Camels were used to travel long distances across the desert to trade.

Carts, drawn by oxen, were not suited to the rocky hill tracks of Palestine, but they were sometimes used to carry farm produce.

TRAVEL FOR THE RICH

In New Testament times, wealthy and important people travelled by four-wheeled horse-drawn chariots. Very rich people could hire a two-wheeled chariot called an essedom, and drive themselves.

The most luxurious way to travel was in a litter carried by slaves.

You can read more about travel on the page on Letters.

Bible Search

- Road repairing: *Isaiah 62:10*

- Robbers on the road: *Luke 10:30*

- Donkey transport: *1 Samuel 25:18–25*

TRAVEL BY SEA

Many Jews were frightened of the power of the sea. If you escaped being shipwrecked, then you risked being killed by pirates. Usually, the only people who travelled by sea were soldiers and traders. The Egyptians and Phoenicians were skilled boat-builders.

SOLOMON'S NAVY

Only one king of Israel ever built a navy: King Solomon. To do this, Solomon made a deal with the best sailors and boat-builders around: the Phoenicians.

FISHING BOATS

The Sea of Galilee is not a sea but a large inland lake. When Jesus wanted to cross to the other side, he went by fishing boat. All fishing boats had oars, and some had sails. Jesus and his twelve disciples could just squash into one boat. To find out more, turn to the page on Fishing.

A pirate

- Solomon's ships:
I Kings 10:22

- Paul's sea trip to Rome:
Acts 27:1–44; 28:11–13

- Paul's adventures at sea:
2 Corinthians 11:25–26

- Jesus in a storm:
Mark 4:35–41

Bible Search

PAUL AT SEA

Paul had some hair-raising experiences at sea. Luke's account of the time Paul was shipwrecked is one of the best descriptions of a sea journey in ancient literature.

Paul would have travelled on a grain ship. It would have had a sculpted figure on the bow (front), representing the name of the ship. Sailors liked to think their boats were people. Often they painted an eye on each side of the bow.

A central mast supported a square mainsail and a small topsail. A small sail at the front, called a foresail, was used to help with steering.

The back of the ship, called the stern, was often built up into the shape of a goose's neck, topped with a goose's head.

Two large oars in the stern took the place of an underwater rudder. There were three heavy anchors.

CREW AND PASSENGERS

There were no passenger ships. Travellers slept on the deck of cargo ships, and brought their own mattresses, food and crockery. There were 276 people on Paul's ship.

There were no compasses. The captain judged his position by the stars.

Travellers brought their own mattresses

TREES IN THE BIBLE

Many hills in Israel that are bare today were covered with woods in Bible times. Trees were important for building and making furniture. Some trees were important as a source of food, especially fruit trees. 'When you capture a city… do not cut down its fruit trees,' said the laws given by Moses to the Israelites.

FIG
Adam and Eve's first clothes were made from the large leaves of a fig tree. Dried figs were a source of iron in soldiers' rations.

SYCAMORE
(This is a type of fig tree, different to our sycamore tree.) The sycamore was the tree that Zacchaeus climbed to see Jesus. Its branches grew low down, so it was easy to climb.

PALM
This was often used as a symbol for victory. People waved palm leaves when Jesus rode into Jerusalem as their king. Palm trees produced dates: an important food.

CEDAR
The country of Lebanon was famous for its forests of giant cedar trees. The people of Israel thought that this beautiful evergreen tree was the greatest of all trees. The long-lasting, sweet-scented red wood of the cedar was prized for making furniture, carved panelling and important buildings. The cedar did not grow in Israel, so it had to be imported from Lebanon.

OAK
In Old Testament times, many peoples thought that oak trees were holy. Arabs today still prefer to bury their dead under oak trees.

CAROB
This was a common tree. In Jesus' story of the prodigal son, pigs were fed on the sweet bean pods of the carob tree.

The Ark of the Covenant

ACACIA
The acacia was one of the few trees that grew in the desert. Its wood was light and hard-wearing. Acacia was used to make the frame of God's desert worship tent (the Tabernacle) and the Ark of the Covenant.

POPLAR
The Israelites were taken to Babylonia as prisoners. They were too sad to sing in this new place. They hung up their harps on poplar trees, and sat crying by the riverside.

ANY QUESTIONS
1 Why did Zacchaeus choose to climb a sycamore tree to see Jesus?
2 Which trees were used as a source of food?

Bible Search

- Fruit trees: *Deuteronomy 20:19*
- Dried figs: *I Samuel 25:18*
- Palms for victory: *John 12–13*
- A sad song Babylon: *Psalm 137:2*

The Israelites were very welcoming

VISITORS

A WELCOME FOR STRANGERS

In the time of Abraham, the Israelites lived in tents in the desert area of Canaan, which was a vast, lonely, dangerous place. The Israelites thought it their duty to welcome travellers. It was considered evil to turn someone away, as he might die in the desert from a lack of food and water. From this time on, welcoming visitors became a custom.

IN A RUSH

Abraham was sitting at the opening of his tent when three strangers came into view. He rushed to meet them, but didn't ask them their names, as this would not have been polite. Abraham quickly chose one of his best calves, and his servant hurried to prepare a meal for the guests.

GREETINGS

When an important visitor arrived, the host made a low bow. Friends were kissed on both cheeks. Water was then provided to wash the visitor's hot, dusty feet. Refreshing, perfumed oil might be poured on the guest's head.

A meal was prepared and served, and the host stood while his guest ate. Introductions were only made at the end of the meal.

The host bowed when visitors arrived

Visitors' feet were washed

Bible Search

- Abraham: *Genesis 18:1–15*
- Moses: *Exodus 2:15–17*
- A neighbour: *Luke 11:5–13*
- Welcome visitors: *Romans 12:13; Hebrews 13:2*

STRANGERS IN TOWN

In Old Testament times, there were no inns or cafes. Later, there were some inns, but most were not pleasant places. A stranger arriving in town would sit by the town well, or by the city gates, and wait to be invited to someone's home.

A stranger by a well

HELP!

Jesus told a story about a man who had an unexpected visitor late at night. To his horror, he discovered that he had no food to offer his guest. He rushed to his neighbour and woke him up. He would not go away until his angry neighbour gave him some bread. (Jesus used the story to show that God answers our prayers!)

A visitor who stayed more than two or three days was expected to contribute towards the cost of food.

WASHING AND TOILETS

Keeping clean was very important. Jewish teachers taught that to wash well was better than any medicine. Washing helped to prevent the spread of diseases. The Romans brought sewage systems and public baths to Palestine.

TOILETS AND DRAINS

Toilets did not have pipes leading to underground sewers. In towns, people emptied buckets into gutters, and the sewage drained away in open drains. But the Romans did have sewage systems. King Herod rebuilt Caesarea and Samaria using Roman towns as his model for a sewage system. Near Caesarea, archaeologists have found pipes which emptied sewage into the sea. There was also a drainage and sewage system in Herod's Temple in Jerusalem. Toilets were 'flushed' by a small stream which flowed under them.

Bible Search

- Abraham's first words to his visitors: *Genesis 18:3-5*
- Rudeness to Jesus: *Luke 7:44*
- Kinds of soap: *Jeremiah 2:22*

The ruins of Herod's bathhouse

FOOT WASHING

Today, when people come in from a journey, they often freshen up by washing their hands and face. In Bible times, people washed their feet. It was extremely bad manners not to wash the feet of your guests. If you were rich enough to have a slave, this would be the slave's job.

BATHING

Bathing was done at the public baths, if the town had one, or in the river or a spring. By the time of the New Testament, more and more towns followed the Roman custom and built public baths.

People also washed as a sign that they wanted to be fit to worship God. You can read more about this on the page on Worship.

CLEANING TEETH

There were no toothbrushes. 'Scented pepper' was used to sweeten the breath. This was probably a variety of aniseed.

SOAP

A very rough soap was made from sodium carbonate and fat, or fat mixed with the ashes of plants that had soda in them. To make themselves smell nice, people rubbed herbs, such as rosemary or marjoram, on their bodies.

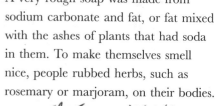

Water pots

WATER
FOR LIFE

There was no rain at all from June to September. In October and March, there was some heavy rain, but it only lasted for a few days. Light rain fell in hilly areas from October to May. So, there was not much rain, and water was very precious. The lives of the people depended on springs, wells and streams.

- Friendship: *John 4:7-15*
- Hezekiah's tunnel: *2 Chronicles 32:30-31*
- Enemies: *Genesis 26:15*
- A well-digging song: *Numbers 21:17-18*

KING HEZEKIAH'S TUNNEL

Jerusalem had no spring. People had to go outside the city to get water. King Hezekiah was worried that if an enemy army surrounded the city, they would be cut off from their supply of water. So he instructed his builders to cut an underground tunnel through solid rock. His workmen started digging from both ends and met in the middle. You can still see the tunnel today. It was a brilliant piece of engineering.

WELLS

In the earliest times written about in the Old Testament, no one had found a way of storing large supplies of water. It had to be fetched from a well in jars. Every town had many wells. Older girls were often given the job of collecting well water.

A quick way of declaring war was to fill your enemies' wells with earth and rocks.

CISTERNS

A cistern was a pear-shaped pit for holding water. At first, cisterns were cut out of limestone rock. Later, people found out how to dig pits in the ground and waterproof them with plaster made from lime.

MAKING FRIENDS

Do you want to show you are friends with someone? Today you might say, 'Have a sweet.' In Bible times you asked for, or offered, a drink of water.

UNDERGROUND POOLS

In New Testament times, some towns had giant man-made pools, or reservoirs. The water from the reservoirs flowed to the towns through canals and stone or clay pipes.

The Romans built aqueducts (canals that went over bridges) to bring water from mountain springs to the towns.

WEATHER
AND TIME

There were only two named seasons: the cold, wet winter, called the rainy season, and the hot, dry summer, called the dry season. There were twelve months in a year. By the time of the New Testament, the Jews followed the Babylonian system of naming the months.

The cold, wet winter

The hot, dry summer

YEARS

Every country had its own system for dating years. This was rather confusing. At first the Jews used important events, or the reign of kings, as a dating system. In Jesus' time, some Jews dated the years from the date the Romans took over the land. Other people dated time from the year we would call 3761 BC, when they thought the world began.

MONTHS

For the Jews, a month began on the first day of the new moon, which gave 354 days a year. This was too short, because the Earth takes 365 days to go round the sun. So every few years, the Jews added an extra month.

A new moon

DAYS AND WEEKS

A week of seven days goes back to the very earliest times, and was made law by Moses. A new day began at sunset, when the day's work was over. Every seventh day was called 'the Sabbath', and the day before was 'the Preparation'. Other days were known by numbers: the first day of the week, the second, and so on.

A new day began at sunset

- New Year's Day: *Leviticus 23:24*
- Hours: *Matthew 20:1–6*
- Dates: *Amos 1:1*
- Days: *Matthew 27:62; 28:1*

HOURS

There were no hours in Old Testament times. Time was described more generally, such as morning, middle of the day, or the time of the evening sacrifice.

When Jesus was alive, a day was divided into twelve hours. Because daylight lasted longer in summer, an hour in summer was longer than an hour in winter.

Nights were not divided into hours but into 'watches', that is, a fixed period of time when a sentry was on duty. In New Testament times, there were four watches in a night: evening, midnight, cockcrow and dawn.

The Greeks and Romans told the time with sundials or with water clocks.

A sentry on watch duty

Spinning

WEAVERS
AND CLOTH

Clothes were made from wool

In Bible times, most everyday clothes were made from wool. Many women made their own clothes. Sometimes they made the material too, by spinning wool into thread, dyeing it, and weaving it into cloth!

A long spindle was used to spin the wool into thick thread. The spindle was a stick of wood with a hook at one end and a whorl (a heavy stone or piece of clay) at the other.

EMBROIDERY

Clothes were often decorated with embroidery, and the Jews were probably very skilled at this work. Complicated patterns were stitched in the popular colours of green, black, yellow and red. Gold thread, made from real gold, was sometimes used. Archaeologists have found many needles used for this type of work. In the Bible, the word 'embroidery' may also discribe patterns made as the material was woven, or quilting and tapestry work.

FULLER

A fuller's job was to wash wool and cloth. When a fleece was shorn from a sheep, it needed a good cleaning. The fuller dipped the material in water, beat it, washed it and bleached it in the sun. Fullers worked outside the town, close to water.

DYEING

Often, thread was left in its natural colours of white, brown and black. Sometimes it was dyed. The most expensive colour was purple. Purple was a sign of power, and religious teachers did not approve of it.

WEAVING

Nearly every home had a loom for weaving cloth. Early looms were horizontal, and were pegged out on the ground. The shuttle which held the thread was passed from side to side, first of all going over and then under the large warp (vertical) threads. Later, vertical looms were invented, and weights were attached to the warp threads to keep them taut.

Bible Search

- Purple cloth:
  Acts 16:14

- Jesus' seamless tunic:
  John 19:23–24

- Embroidery:
  Exodus 26:36; 39:3

A fuller

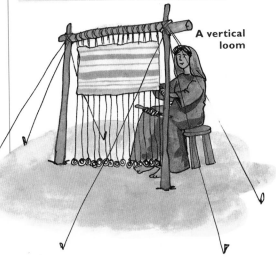

A vertical loom

WEDDINGS
A BUSINESS DEAL

A marriage was a business deal fixed up between two families. Love came second. Girls could be betrothed when they were about thirteen, and boys at about fourteen. Often, they were married a year later.

AGREEING THE PRICE

The girl's family lost a worker when she left home to marry. So the boy's family paid a 'bride price'. There were long talks about payment.

A betrothal was more like a marriage than an engagement. A betrothal could only be broken by legal means, similar to a divorce.

PRESENTS

A father gave his daughter a present, perhaps servants or land. The groom gave the bride jewellery and clothes. In New Testament times, this included a circlet of silver coins, which was fastened to the bride's headdress.

THE WEDDING

Weddings were not all alike, but this is what often happened. Before the wedding, a contract was drawn up and signed or spoken before witnesses. The best man, called the 'friend of the bridegroom', was in charge. He had to make sure that everything went smoothly.

WEDDING CLOTHES

The bride and groom were dressed in rich clothes. The bridesmaids braided the bride's hair with jewels. The bride and groom wore crowns of flowers. The bride wore a veil. Sometimes guests were given wedding clothes to wear.

Braiding the bride's hair

THE EVENING BEFORE THE WEDDING

The groom and his friends came to the bride's house. Her parents 'gave her away' with a prayer. There was a torchlit procession to the groom's home, with tambourines, singing and dancing. Later, the bride went to her room with her bridesmaids, while the groom had a party.

THE WEDDING DAY

The groom spent the day merrymaking and playing games with his friends. Sometime during the evening, he came for his bride.

A great feast was held for all the guests. The bride and groom sat under a canopy decorated with flowers. They were treated like royalty.

The bride and groom spent their first night together in a specially decorated 'bridal room'. There was no honeymoon, but the feasting went on for a week.

Bible Search

- Foolish bridesmaids *Matthew 25:1-13*
- A near disaster at a wedding: *John 2:1-11*
- Wedding guests: *Matthew 22:1-12*

WEIGHTS AND MEASURING

Our modern Bibles translate the measurements of Bible times into terms we understand, so we don't have to struggle with mental arithmetic. The first weights were stones. Distances could be measured by arrows, donkeys and soldiers.

Oxen ploughing

YOU CHEAT!

In Old Testament times, weights were not exact, and it was easy for traders to cheat people. Careful shoppers carried their own weights about with them so they could check what they were sold. By the time of the New Testament, weights had become more standard, and a different system of weights and measurements was in use.

WEIGHTS

The first weights were stones. Archaeologists have found hundreds of small stones with weights marked on them. Later, bronze and lead weights were used. Weights were sometimes carved into animal shapes: these were easy to recognise and handle.

The most common weight was the shekel, which was used to weigh silver. The heaviest weight was the talent.

Weighing was done on scales. Before coins were invented, silver was weighed on scales and used as money.

Scales

Money stones

MEASURING

In the Old Testament, the unit of measurement was the human body!
- A cubit was 445 mm (17 1/2 in)
- A finger was 19 mm (3/4 in)
- A palm was 76 mm (3 in)
- A span was 230 mm (9 in)

Palm

DISTANCES

In the Old Testament, a distance was measured by how far an arrow could be shot, or how far a caravan of donkeys could travel in a day. A day's journey was about 28 km (18 miles).

ROMAN MILES

The word 'mile' comes from the Latin word for a thousand. It referred to the distance covered by a marching soldier: one thousand paces was about 1,478 meters (4,849 ft.). A pace was the distance covered by a left and a right step.

Measuring distance

Marching soldiers

OTHER MEASUREMENTS

Farmland was measured by how much land two oxen yoked together could plough in one day.

Water was measured in fathoms. A fathom was 2 m (6 ft).

A caravan of donkeys

Foods and drinks were measured in containers: pots, baskets or by the donkey-load.

- An attempt at a common standard: *Genesis 23:16*
- Cheating: *Micah 6:11*
- An arrow shot: *Genesis 21:16*
- A day's donkey ride: *Jonah 3:3*

Bible Search

77

WORSHIP IN BIBLE TIMES

F or the Jews, religion was a way of life, not just reserved for special times when they went to the Temple or the synagogue. Laws about matters such as the food they could or couldn't eat, showed that every part of life belonged to God.

Bible Search

- Singing at family worship: *Mark 14:26*
- Music in Temple worship: *Psalm 150; 1 Chronicles 25:6–7*
- Guest preacher: *Luke 4:16–21*
- A family sacrifice: *Luke 2:22–24*

PRAYER

Three times a day, in the morning, at midday and in the evening, every adult male Jew stopped what he was doing. He had to turn towards the Temple in Jerusalem and say the Shema (Deuteronomy 6:4-9 and 11:13-21; Numbers 15:37-41). Women, slaves and children did not do this.

There were also set prayers, called the eighteen blessings, which were said two or three times a day. Prayers were usually spoken aloud with hands raised to God, while standing or kneeling.

When they prayed, men wore a prayer shawl with long fringes, and a phylactery (a small box containing Bible verses).

A priest

TEMPLE

Every morning and evening at the Temple, a priest sacrificed a lamb. Then he stood on the steps above the Men's Court. He recited the Shema and read aloud a passage from the Law (the first five books of the Bible).

At three o'clock every day, a priest took a short service which included a Bible reading and prayers. Sometimes a choir chanted psalms and played music.

Thousands of people went to the Temple to pray. They bought lambs or pigeons from the Temple traders to make their own private sacrifices.

(See also the pages on Sacrifices and on Festivals.)

SYNAGOGUE

An hour-long service was held each Sabbath in every synagogue. There were opening prayers, including the Shema and the eighteen blessings. These were followed by a reading from the Law, which was divided into 153 parts, with a set reading for each Sabbath.

There was a reading from the prophets, which was then discussed. Often the congregation chanted psalms. The service ended with prayers and a collection of money.

Stopping work to pray

A lamb and pigeons for sacrifice

Chanting psalms

ANY QUESTIONS
1 How and where did people pray?
2 How did people worship on the Sabbath?

ZEALOTS
AND OTHER GROUPS

In every country, people belong to different religions and political parties. Some people feel very strongly about the political party they belong to, but many other people are busy with their own lives, and don't get involved. It was just the same in the time of Jesus.

SADDUCEES

The Sadducees were small in number, but had a lot of power because they were the ruling party in the Sanhedrin. The Sadducees came from the wealthy families of Jerusalem.

Most of the priests were Sadducees. They liked the Romans, and saw Jesus as a threat. They were worried that if Jesus started a riot, the Romans would blame them for not keeping order, and then they would lose their jobs.

The Sadducees saw Jesus as a threat

- Sicarii: *Acts 21:38*
- Jesus for king: *John 6:14–15*
- Deserting Jesus: *John 6:66*
- Herodians: *Mark 12:13*
- Sadducees: *Mark 12:18*

ZEALOTS

Zealots were terrorist freedom fighters. They wanted to get rid of the Romans by force. In the time of Jesus, there were lots of small groups who often fought each other as well as the Romans. One fierce group was called the Sicarii, which meant 'dagger men'.

Many zealots came from Galilee. At first, they supported Jesus, until they found he didn't want to lead an armed rebellion against Rome.

Zealots

ESSENES

The Essenes move to the desert

Essenes also hated the Romans, but instead of fighting, they went away and set up small communities in the desert. One group lived to the north-west of the Dead Sea.

APOCALYPTISTS

Apocalyptists thought that very soon there would be a great battle, when God would put an end to the evil in the world. They wrote books describing their weird visions and dreams about future events.

The Apocalyptists wrote books

HERODIANS

Herodians were a group of people in Galilee who were friends of Herod Antipas. Herod was kept in power by the Romans, so the Herodians supported Rome. They were against Jesus, because they thought he was a dangerous troublemaker.